Fighting for Your Children

FIGHTING FOR YOUR CHILDREN.

(A Father's Guide to Custody)

John Steinbreder
(Richard G. Kent, Esq)

TAYLOR PUBLISHING COMPANY
DALLAS, TEXAS

Published by Taylor Publishing Company

1550 West Mockingbird Lane

Dallas, Texas 75235

Book design by Mark McGarry

Set in Walbaum

Library of Congress Cataloging-in-Publication Data

Steinbreder, John.

Fighting for your children : a father's guide to

navigating the system / John Steinbreder and Richard Kent, Esq.

p. cm. Includes index.

ISBN 0-97833-941-8

1. Custody of chilren–United States–Popular works.

2. Father'–Legal status, laws, etc.–United States–Popular works.

3. Father and child–United States.

I. Kent, Richard, G. II. Title.

KF547.Z9S74   1998

346.7301'73–dc21   97-45944

CIP

Printed in the United States of America

10   9   8   7   6   5   4   3   2   1

For our daughters – Exa, Lindsay, and Sarah

CONTENTS

Foreword

Addressing a joint meeting of Congress almost half a century ago, General Douglas MacArthur said, "In war, there is no substitute for victory." He was speaking, of course, about the political turmoil surrounding America's conduct in the Korean War. But could he just as readily have been addressing the personal "wars" now overwhelming our society in fights over child custody? If so, the brilliant general would have badly misspoken, for in family law disputes, no one ever wins. Victory in a custody battle is an impossibility. The only triumph occurs when parents can put aside their differences to work with a semblance of emotional and intellectual harmony toward their children's development.

We are in a time of great social transition, perhaps the most rapid and radical in recorded history. The ideals and expectations we held regarding marriage and parenting, even as recently as 1951 when General MacArthur was addressing Congress, have undergone a sea of change. Everything now seems upside down. Expectations no longer meet reality; role models no longer meet expectations; problems no longer meet solutions; and the "best interests" of children are suddenly placed on a par with the "rights" of their parents. How to deal with or even understand all of this is the overriding call of our times.

In this context, a book telling fathers how to fight for their children is a battle manual for a war that should never have to be waged. Children should not be treated as assets to be won or lost or as territory to be claimed or relinquished. Not even the semantics of battle should have a place in matters of child custody and visitation arising from divorce. That is, if we lived in an ideal world.

The trouble is that we live in the real world, a place where people don't always behave as they should. Courts are crowded and overwhelmed, laws are many and twisted, and children are sometimes wronged and injured. So, for better or worse, a how-to manual about fighting for your sons and daughters is still necessary. And the pages that follow offer a thoughtful and comprehensive treatment on the subject.

It is a burden of our times that, although great attention is paid toward attaining the commendable goal of gender equality, little effort is devoted to understanding gender differences in parenting or even to examining whether differences exist beyond the most obvious ones related to physiology. If it "takes a village" to raise a child, can we accept that a child may be lawfully deprived of even a portion of either parent's presence without suffering an irremedial loss? Wise courts dealing with divorce recognize this impossibility and increasingly adopt procedures to encourage parents to deal constructively with one another and maximize coparenting and collaborative activites. Those are critical goals, and this book speaks clearly about their importance. But, at the same time, it also addresses those situations in which parents, for whatever reasons, cannot work together. Perhaps such incompatibility is our fault as a society. We often give the wrong messages. Worse, we stand silent in the face of chaos. Perhaps what is needed is a training program in interpersonal relations that begins at the age of three. Perhaps there should be new paradigms for courtship and marriage, teaching from the outset that fighting over the sharing of a child after a divorce is unacceptable conduct. Maybe what we adults need is peer pressure to grow up.

Until that ideal moment arrives, however, we are left with only the reality. In that reality some courts, lawyers, and lawmakers—but thankfully not all—are insensitive to the fact that a child will forever have two biological parents and that each one will make an indelible impact on the child's life.

This book is designed to give at least one of those parents—the father—some guidance as he stumbles through the maze of organized conflict that surrounds a contest over custody. And it does it well. Paradoxically, most of the advice you'll find within could just as easily be written for a mother seeking custody. It's not an issue of gender, it's a matter of maturity. Family laws and rules are generally intended to be gender neutral. That they may be perceived otherwise or applied by a judge or lawyer with bias is obviously an unacceptable deviation. The problem, of course, is that when a deviation occurs in your case, it is devastating. You do not want to hope for a correction or wind up as a statistic in someone's polemic about what is wrong with the judicial system. You want things to go right for you from the start.

Many times they don't. The hope is that by reading this book and following its sage advice, you will be able to guide yourself more wisely through the process and have a better chance of making sure that the result is in the best interest of your child. That is what the court system is all about and, believe it or not, that is what it often delivers. The true test is in your hands.

IRA LURVEY

Ira Lurvey is a Los Angeles attorney who headed the American Bar Association's Family Law Section in 1996–1997 and who previously chaired the Family Law sections of the California State Bar and the Los Angeles County Bar. He writes and lectures nationally on family law.

ACKNOWLEDGMENTS

A project of this magnitude would never have been completed without the good work and loyal support of several colleagues and friends. First of all, our thanks to agents Frank Coffey and Frank Weimann, who believed in this book from the beginning and were able to help make it happen, and to Mike Emmerich, who had the vision to get it started. We also appreciate the efforts of Taylor publisher Lynn Brooks and editor Jason Rath in producing such an important and attractive volume and making sure it gets into all the right stores.

Several people helped us put together the stories, statistics, and other information this book holds, and we'd like to thank them as well. Linda Kelly read the manuscript before anyone else and made several insightful comments that improved the finished product. She also let us bounce ideas off her along the way and was always supportive. Judge Joseph L. Steinberg shared many of his worthy ideas on the subject, as did attorney Rob Skovgaard, psychologist Susan Freedland, and Janet Esposito Daigle, the chief of the Family Relations Department in Bridgeport, Connecticut. We were also fortunate to have the input of child psychiatrist Stephen Herman, who has written a marvelous book entitled *Parent vs. Parent: How You and Your Child Can Survive the Custody Battle.* Our conversations with Dr. Herman, who is a court-appointed expert in custody disputes, proved invaluable, and we were also happy to have his publication nearby. In addition, we appreciated the time other judges, lawyers, therapists, and social workers gave us as we researched this project, and the trust they put in us to respect their privacy. Similar thanks to the fathers who related their often horrific experiences on the child custody battlefield and to Ira Lurvey for penning the foreword.

We referred to a number of first-rate books and periodicals in preparing this publication. In addition to Dr. Herman's treatise, we relied on the work of Louis Kiefer, who wrote *How to Win Custody*; Robert Bernstein and Richard Worth, who published the *Divorced Dad's Handbook*; Timothy J. Horgan, who authored *Winning Your Divorce*; and Joseph Goldstein, Albert Solini, Sonja Goldstein and Anna Freud, who put together *The Best Interests of the Child.* We are also appreciative of the research done by the School of Family Studies at the University of Connecticut as well as the coverage several newspapers, magazines, and newsletters have given the subject of custody, including *Time, Newsweek, The New York Times, USA Today*, the *ABA Journal*, the *ABA's Family Advocate*, the *Connecticut Family Lawyer*, the *Wall Street Journal, Parents, Good Housekeeping*, and the *Father's National Review.*

On a personal note, Richard would like to thank his assistant Jennifer Mengold; his associate Jocelyn Hurwitz; his partner at Cohen & Wolf, Rick Albrecht; and his wife, Lisa Kasden Kent. And John would like to extend his gratitude to Eric Copage of *The New York Times Magazine* for encouraging, editing, and running his About Men column; Jerry Tarde and his colleagues at *Golf Digest* for all those terrific assignments; Mark McCormack and Mark Reiter of the International Management Group for their help and support; Duncan Christy of *Sky* for the classy way he runs his magazines; Robin McMillan of *Met Golfer* for another fun year of work; Geoff Russell of *Golf World* for getting him involved with that publication; Dave Seanor of *GOLFWEEK* and Cindi Crain of *Golf & Travel* for the places they send him; Chuck Wechsler of *Sporting Classics* for letting him write about duck hunting, his favorite sport; and his friends at ESPN for putting his work on TV. In addition, he would like to thank Dr. Joanna Whitcup for her help not only in flushing out some key points in this book but also in getting him through some of the tougher times of the past several years, and Charlie Monagan of *Connecticut Magazine* for allowing him to use parts of a profile he wrote on Judge Steinberg. John would also like to express his appreciation to Harvey and Sarah Morse and Debbie and Jonathon Armerding for letting him work on this opus at their dining room tables when he was on the road last spring, as well as to the many friends and family members—from his cowboy kin in West Texas to his childhood buddies in Fairfield, Connecticut—who supported him so completely during his times of need. He is grateful for the way he and his former wife, Christie, are able to parent together and thanks her for the respect and cooperation she so often shows. And finally, he would like to pay tribute to his daughter, Exa, a bright and cheerful six-year-old whose capacity to love and understand—even in the middle of a couple of book projects—knows no bounds.

INTRODUCTION

This is a book we have wanted to write for some time. Richard's interest stems mostly from his work over the past two decades as a matrimonial lawyer, though as the divorced father of two, he has some understanding of the issues on a personal level as well. As a journalist who writes mostly about sports and business, I didn't have any involvement with the topic professionally until my daughter, now six, became the subject of a custody dispute between my former wife and me. But then I started doing what writers frequently do, which is putting down on paper the important things that happen in their lives. And nothing had ever been more important to me.

Richard and I first met when I asked him to represent me in my custody case, and not surprisingly, we spent a lot of time together during the process. One of the things we talked about most often was the inherent prejudices the legal system has against fathers when it comes to custody, child support, and visitation. The whole process appeared skewed in favor of women, and the more we looked into it, the stronger the evidence bore that out. Richard remembered the many cases he had handled over the years in which fathers lost financially and emotionally taxing battles for their children simply because they were men. He also heard countless stories from lawyers and other colleagues in the legal profession who had been involved with similarly one-sided fights. As for me, I had several male friends relate their often harrowing experiences with family courts after they heard about my situation. Richard and I wondered whether there were any books dealing with custody from a man's perspective, and to our surprise, we found none. The more we thought about it, the more it seemed we were on to something.

We became much more convinced after I wrote a piece about divorce and custody for the About Men column in *The New York Times Magazine.* The response was tremendous, and many fathers wrote or called to relate heart-wrenching tales about how they had fought for their kids and to decry a system that had treated them unfairly. Suddenly, it seemed a subject that men wanted to talk about and one that touched them in very emotional and personal ways. So not long after that story ran in the spring of 1994, Richard and I put together a book proposal and secured a contract with Taylor Publishing. Our haphazard discussions had turned into something tangible and good.

One of our aims in this book is to help men understand the legal process as it relates to custody battles so they can enjoy greater success when they find themselves fighting for their kids. It is by no means a screed against women or a manual on how spiteful fathers can wrest custody away from former spouses and perfectly capable mothers. Rather, we see it as a guide designed to assist men with custody issues that are unique to their gender and to help them deal with a system that is often tilted against fathers. Most of all, we hope the book will give fathers a fair shot at maintaining the best possible relationship with their children even when their marriage has fallen apart.

Men haven't always needed so much help. Laws in ancient Rome gave fathers complete control over their children, and the rest of Europe treated their youngsters that way for several hundred years after that. But by the mid-nineteenth century, mothers on both sides of the Atlantic had gradually come to be seen as the preferred custodians. Part of the reason for that shift was the dramatic change in the lives of the fathers. In Colonial America, for example, men were expected not only to provide for and protect their children but also to help teach them and guide them as they grew up. Fathers were active parents in every sense of the word. But then came the Industrial Revolution, and men began leaving their farms and home shops for factories and offices. As a result, most of the child-rearing duties fell to the mothers.

As the pendulum swung in favor of women, the courts began employing what became known as the "tender years" doctrine, based on the presumption that children under the ages of seven or eight would be better raised by their mothers. And things remained that way until the latter part of this century, when that school of thought, thankfully, started to fall out of favor. Though born of good intentions, it had served to almost completely eliminate fathers as an option when it came to custody considerations. The "tender years" principle is no longer legally recognized, but we suspect that some judges, attorneys, and social workers still believe in it. In its place, the courts are now

evoking the "best interests" doctrine, which decrees that custody should be given to the parent who can best meet the children's needs. A vast improvement, to be sure, but the criteria for
determining exactly what those needs are and how they can
best be served are extremely vague. There is plenty of room for
interpretation, which also means that there is great potential for
confusion. Still, it is a step in the right direction for men, who
have also been helped by the fact that record numbers of
women have now entered the work force. No longer is it so easy
for mothers to argue that they should be the custodial parents
because they are more available. And with more fathers than
ever before fighting to be a bigger part of their children's lives
and to protect their parental rights, the pendulum is actually
swinging back toward center. Here's hoping it eventually finds
the middle ground where fathers are given equal respect and
consideration as parents.

In writing this book, we frequently used the personal pro-
noun *he* instead of the combination *he or she* for simplicity's
sake. It was not meant to reflect any gender bias, and we obviously believe that men and women are equally capable as
judges, lawyers, social workers, and of course, parents. We also
need to point out that the names of the men, women, and children who are the subjects or litigants in custody battles have
been changed throughout to protect their identities and respect
their wishes for privacy. In addition, you should be aware that
although we do provide some legal advice, we recommend that
you consult your own attorney before taking any action. There
are no national divorce laws that lay out blanket procedures,

and the principles regarding divorce and custody, which are different in the individual states, change frequently.

And finally, we feel a need to explain our use of *battle* and *fight* in the book. As we were researching this volume, some of our sources criticized us for employing those words so often, saying they perpetuate the stereotype of all divorces and custody cases as full-fledged wars and encourage men and women to treat them accordingly. If those words weren't used as frequently, the reasoning went, then maybe the disputes wouldn't deteriorate so easily to those conditions. Points well taken. But the fact is, nothing better describes what actually occurs during a custody case. What else is one parent going to do if the other tries to move away with his children or keep him from visiting his sons and daughters? What else is going to happen between two people who love their children and who each believe they can provide the better home? Of course they will fight, and of course they will battle. The more important issue is how the parents conduct themselves during those difficult times. We argue throughout this publication that men should take the high road whenever possible; that they should treat their former spouses with consideration and respect; and, most of all, that they should be sure what they do is truly in the best interests of the children.

As far as we're concerned, it's the only way to go.

JOHN STEINBREDER

EASTON, CONNECTICUT

JANUARY 1998

1

What Fathers Are Facing

Bob Jenkins got divorced three years ago and worked out a joint custody agreement that enabled him to spend every other weekend and most summers with his three daughters, ages six, eight, and eleven. As a man who had played an active role in their care and upbringing, Bob was disappointed at not having more days with his girls. But he truly believed they would be better served living most of the time with their mother. She worked part time and continued to live in the only house their children had ever known, while he toiled long hours as an investment banker and traveled frequently. Also, he had just moved into an inexpensive rental cottage that didn't have much room.

"I was wiped out financially from the divorce and needed some time to get back on my feet," Bob explains. "Until I was able to do that, I thought it was best for my ex-wife to be the primary parent because I could not provide as stable and comfortable a home."

Two years later, however, Bob began to reassess his position. He had left his banking firm and set up his own investment business, which he operated out of a larger house he had bought a few miles from where his former spouse lived. About the same time he discovered that his former wife had begun drinking heavily and was frequently sharing her home with a man he did not approve of, and whom the children did not like. "I thought the boyfriend and the drinking might be having some adverse effects on my daughters," Bob explains. "I also found that my new job gave me a lot more free time. After thinking about it for a while, I decided to ask my ex-wife if we could make some changes in our custody and visitation arrangement so that I could be with the children more often. She was still pretty bitter about the divorce and didn't like dealing with me a lot. But I figured she would be reasonable about this because I was only asking for an extra weekend or so a month."

Unfortunately, she turned him down flat. Discouraged by her reaction, Bob phoned his attorney, who suggested he approach her one more time. If she still didn't want to alter the agreement, he said, they would go to the courts for help. Bob spoke to his former spouse again, but she remained steadfast. "So I told her that I was going to try and get a judge to modify our visitation arrangement," he says. "I didn't want to fight anymore, but I felt it was my only recourse."

Bob was preparing for his day in court when he received a frantic telephone call from his attorney. His ex-wife had accused him of sexually abusing his youngest daughter during a recent weekend visit and had reported her claim to the child's doctor, her elementary school principal, and the police. In addition, her attorney had made a motion in court to restrict any direct contact between Bob and his children. Though the judge had no concrete evidence of sexual abuse, he ruled without a hearing that Bob could only have supervised telephone conversations with his daughters pending an investigation.

Bob fought the judge's decision and eventually had it overturned, primarily because the court never found that any abuse had occured. But it was only a Pyrrhic victory. Bob had spent nearly $100,000 on legal fees and had gone an entire year without seeing his girls alone. Not surprisingly, the battle took an enormous toll on him emotionally and devastated his children, who had not only been caught in the middle of a terrible fight between their parents but had also been given strong reasons, however unfounded, to distrust their father. "Even though I was cleared, I've never felt that they were completely sure that nothing happened," Bob says. "Three years have gone by, and it's still a bit uncomfortable for all of us. I'm worried that my children will spend the rest of their lives wondering whether it was their mother or me who was telling the truth."

The tragic story of Bob Jenkins sounds too horrible to be believed, but it is true. In fact, fathers have to fight off such accusations all the time. Timothy Horgan cites a study in his fine book, *Winning Your Divorce,* indicating that thirty percent of all custody cases in the United States involve allegations of sexual or physical abuse by the father. And virtually all of those claims are made after the father makes some attempt to modify custody or visitation arrangements. In addition, some experts find that the number of abuse accusations has grown steadily over the past decade. "It's the biggest change I've noticed in fifteen years of practice," says Dr. Stephen Herman, a child and adolescent psychiatrist who often serves as a custody expert for courts in New York and Connecticut. "Either it's an outright allegation of abuse or an inference of sexually inappropriate behavior, usually brought by the mother against the father. I have no idea what percent of those allegations are true, but I do know that they are being made more and more often."

Although there certainly are times when fathers are guilty of such actions, many of the sexual abuse claims have no basis in fact and are only the vindictive work of mothers trying to "beat" their ex-husbands in custody disputes. But such are the obstacles many fathers must overcome as they fight to be with their children.

It seems that no matter how much progress has been made in recent years with respect to fathers' rights, when it comes to custody battles, men are still at a distinct disadvantage. A father's need to be with his children is frequently not taken into consideration, and his children's need to be with him is too often ignored. His career and stereotypes based on his gender are constantly used against him. He is subjected to terrible prejudices. He is left unprotected against the worst kind of terror tactics. And he often loses the right to be the kind of parent he wants to be simply because he is a man.

The Plight of Fathers

It's important to note at this point that not all divorces end up becoming full-fledged custody disputes. And even for those that do, a vast majority are settled out of court by the parents involved. Cases that can't be settled are decided by a judge. Generally speaking, the dispute in a custody case centers on where the children will live and who will watch over them. In some cases, a parent receives sole custody, which means he or she will have primary physical custody of the children as well as the right to make all major decisions regarding their upbringing. And in others, joint custody is the resolution, which mandates that both parents share responsibilities and major decision making for the kids. Either the father or mother may be designated as the primary custodial parent, indicating that he or she is the person with whom the children live a majority of the time. Visitation is almost always granted to parents who have divorced, regardless of their custody status, though the amount of time they may be with their children is unique to each situation. Some share their chldren on a week-to-week or month-to-month basis (known as "split custody"). Others may break it up so that one parent has the children every other weekend, most school vacations, and a month in the summer, while the other parent keeps them the rest of the time. Only in the most extreme circumstances are fathers and mothers denied access to their children altogether, and that usually happens in cases involving violence or abuse.

The legal system as it deals with child custody is supposed to be gender-neutral. But the evidence shows that it is far from fair. According to the American Fathers Coalition, a Washington

D.C. advocacy group, more than ninety percent of all litigated divorces result in the awarding of sole custody to mothers. A 1990 study of divorce in nineteen states by the National Center for Health Statistics found that in seventy-one percent of all litigated and settled cases, mothers received sole custody. Both parents shared custody in 15.5 percent of the disputes, while fathers received sole custody only 8.5 percent of the time. (Friends and relatives took the children in the remainder of the cases.) One study conducted in an urban Ohio county draws on information gathered from 238 randomly selected custody cases involving minor children in which judgments were entered in 1987 and 1988. Fathers received sole custody in only thirteen of those instances, and parents were awarded joint custody in nineteen others. The remaining 206 cases–86.5 percent–were closed with the mother receiving sole custody. In addition, the U.S. Census Bureau found in 1991 that fifty percent of all fathers involved in divorces didn't receive any court-ordered visitation. In researching their 1991 book, *Surviving the Break-Up,* authors Joan Berlin Kelley and Judith Wallerstein discovered that almost half of all the divorced mothers they interviewed saw no value in the father's continued contact with their children. And other studies have claimed that forty percent of all divorced mothers interfere with their children's relationships with their fathers.

For decades judges used the so-called "Tender Years Doctrine" as their basis for awarding sole or primary custody of children to women in all but a few cases with the rationale that a child would be better off with his mother than his father. Officially, that line of reasoning was abandoned in the early

1970s. But it continued in practice for many years. And though the courts today are much more enlightened, they still appear to favor women. Fathers continue to battle the stereotypes of a society that believes a child's place is with the mother and watch as many women manipulate a legal system that often appears stuck in the 1950s.

The famed anthropologist Margaret Mead once said, "Fathers are a biological necessity but a social accident," and it often seems that attitude still exists in the courthouse. Consider what a judge wrote when he ruled on a 1982 custody case: "It would be very difficult for a man to raise two boys like a woman can, therefore I'm going to name [the mother] as managing conservator of the children." Or the thinking of a woman who heads up a state social services department in the Northeast that conducts studies and makes recommendations in custody cases: "Everything being equal with two capable, mature, and loving adults, I believe the mother has a certain sensitivity in specific areas that the father lacks with regard to a young child, and I would come down on her behalf." Or the words of a male judge, thankfully nearing retirement, who says, "Many of us on the bench do have a predisposition for mothers, as long as they are fit, to have custody of a child. In a lot of our eyes, a mother would really have to screw up to lose custody and lose her child." In addition, that judge adds, "I also have a prejudice against little girls being with their father. I bend over backwards to avoid that having an effect on my decisions, but it is a prejudice."

Sadly, there seems to have been a substantial amount of prejudice in the legal system over the years. "One problem has been that the people hearing cases were not only one but sometimes two generations removed from the fathers standing before them," says a forty-year-old female judge. "The vast majority of them were men, and they couldn't imagine others doing what they did not have to do when their children were young." Rob Skovgaard, a veteran attorney based in Stamford, Connecticut, who has represented men, women, and children in custody cases for nearly two decades, has seen men who have found the system so inherently unfair over the years that they have settled before a case ever made it to trial. "They may have had a good argument," Skovgaard explains, "or they really wanted to play that role of primary parent with their children. But they gave up fighting after a while because they felt the deck was stacked against them. The system theoretically is designed to be gender neutral, but at each stop in the process you find out it's really not. The presumption is, and continues to be, being a mother breaks the tie."

BIAS BEYOND THE COURTROOM

Unfortunately, prejudices toward men as capable parents are not just limited to the courthouse. We know of a middle-aged fellow, for example, who attended a dinner party in New York City one night and found himself sitting next to a bright, thoughtful woman who conversed easily on subjects as far-ranging as opera and art, literature and history, politics and sports. The father of two daughters, he was in the midst of a protracted custody battle, and at one point toward the end of the meal his host asked him how he was faring in the courts. Our friend gave a quick update, whereupon his dinner partner suddenly turned to him icily and said: "I can't believe any court would give a man custody of his children over a woman. There's a special bond that develops in the womb between the woman and the child, and that relationship is never surpassed by what goes on with the father. It's just not the same thing." Those surly words quieted the dinner table and shocked most of those in attendance. But the dressing-down didn't phase our friend in the least. "That sort of thing happened to me all the time, and I was used to it," he said later on. "I always believed in what I was doing as a father and was proud to tell people how I was fighting for my children. But after a while I started keeping my custody problems to myself. Most women took offense at what I was doing, no matter how noble or level-headed it might actually have been. They viewed me as some chauvinistic jerk trying to demean motherhood and get back at his ex-wife, when all I was trying to do was stay involved with my children and get equal treatment as a parent. I began to feel I was better off if people just didn't know."

Then there were the troubles of a man who turned to a female lawyer for help when his former wife announced her intentions to move out of state with their six-year-old daughter. The lawyer had handled the couple's divorce in a seemingly fair and even-handed manner that not only saved them thousands of dollars but also enabled them to get through the process with a minimum of rancor and enjoy a civil post-marital relationship. Given that, the man–and his former spouse–quickly turned to her for help when the custody issue came up. "I thought we might be able to work together again," he recalls.

"But during one of our first meetings, the lawyer started talking about possible visitation schedules and told me I would always be entitled to significant amounts of time with my daughter, no matter where she lived, because I was 'pretty good for a father.' The lawyer meant that as a compliment, but it gave me great pause about her objectivity. If she felt that way about men and their parenting abilities, then how could she represent my best interests, or those of my daughter, in this case?"

The couple met with the mediator on several occasions, but it soon became clear that the process would not work this time. So the man informed both the lawyer and his former spouse that he was hiring outside counsel and would fight any proposed move. "The mediator was indignant," he recalls. "She accused me of sabotaging the talks and later recommended several attorneys to my former spouse. She also encouraged my ex-wife to fight for custody of our daughter and later shared with my former spouse's new attorney several bits of potentially damaging personal information she had learned while taking care of our divorce." Fortunately for the father, he prevailed in this case, and his daughter, now ten, lives with him during the school year and spends the summers with her mother. But he still can't get over the reckless disregard that female lawyer had for him and, ultimately, his child, simply because he was a man. "It made the battle twice as expensive and twice as hard emotionally," he says. "And that was unfair to all of us—my daughter, my former wife, and me."

But the battles did not end there. Even after he and his daughter settled into a placid domestic routine after the legal wrangling was over, that same man found himself constantly fighting the prejudices of an uninformed society. When he registered his daughter at an elementary school, he told the administrator that he was divorced and was his daughter's primary custodial parent. "That's fine," said the cheery woman handling the application. "But would you please send us a copy of your custody agreement so that we may have it in our files." The father didn't think anything of the request until he talked to a couple of mothers he knew a few days later, both divorced and with children in the same school. "No one asked for their custody papers," he says. "They wanted mine simply because I was a man."

That same man has had to endure the most common slights from female acquaintances who, after hearing him talk about the difficulties of being the primary parent and wage earner, often say: "Now you know what it's been like for women all these years." Forget, for a moment, that the ones making those remarks in many cases are either completely reliant on their husbands' incomes for support or enjoying significant financial freedom simply because they receive substantial amounts of child support and alimony each month. "What really gets me is they're saying something that would irk them to no end if it was uttered by a man," he explains. "How would a woman feel, for example, if I came up to her in a bar after work one evening, listened for a moment to her talk about what a brutal day she had had at the office and then said, 'Now you know what men have been going through all these years'? She would want to strangle me for making such an inane statement, and I wouldn't blame her one bit. It would be a dumb thing to say, but the fact is, women say things like that to me all the time."

FINANCIAL FRUSTRATIONS

One of the most frustrating by-products of divorces and custody battles is the sense of financial entrapment men often feel. In many cases, fathers are the breadwinners, and the economic onus falls on them. Regardless of who brought the legal action, they are usually the ones responsible for most of the lawyer fees, and then they must shell out hundreds, sometimes thousands, of dollars each month in child support. Very rarely do they receive anything themselves. A 1991 study by the Federal Office of Income Security Policy, for example, found that less than 30 percent of all custodial fathers received a child support award of some sort, while some 80 percent of custodial mothers did.

No one can argue with a system that demands that a parent be financially responsible for his children, but many men find it maddening that that same system does not force a former spouse to account for how she spends child support money. Is the mother using it to buy groceries and clothes for the kids, to pay for ballet classes and summer camp? Or is she actually spending a large portion on herself? Equally distressing are the courts that expect fathers to turn over as much as half of their salaries to their ex-wives without any consideration as to how they can pay their own bills or get back on their feet. Many men in the wake of a divorce or custody battle have a hard time affording suitable living quarters that could accommodate their children for weekend visits, and the hours they have to put in just to keep their heads above water financially hardly allow them much quality time with their kids. In addition, they often find that no amount of child support will give them unfettered access to their children or a strong voice in their upbringing; the same courts that mandate their child support payments are much less rigorous when it comes to enforcing things like visitation schedules. The courts, in many instances, treat fathers more like bankers than parents, making them accountable for financial relief but then relegating them to second-class status when it comes to raising the kids. They frequently feel that they pay way too much and receive way too little in return.

Another problem for men is how their careers and wealth are used against them. Take the case of Jim Bryant, a lawyer who was making nearly $80,000 a year when he and his wife split up. "I had a good job, and that helped my ex-wife get a very generous alimony and child support payment each month," Bryant says. "But she also used it as a way to keep the children from me. We have two kids, a boy and a girl, and any time I made a move to see them more often, she countered with some comment about my working all the time and claimed I couldn't take care of the kids as well as she could because I was so busy with my career. Yet that same career was still giving her a nice lifestyle and the opportunity to parent full time because I was paying all the bills. She would have been furious had I quit my job and done something less demanding so I could spend more time with my children, because it would have meant less money and less control of the kids for her. She wanted it both ways, and guess what? That's what she got."

The primary issue here is one of choice—and a father's ability to decide how to balance his professional and personal life. If he determines that it is in his best interest to work seventy hours a week and be less available for his kids so that he can provide a better lifestyle and education for them, then that should be his option. But the same should apply if he wants to cut back on his office hours—and most likely his income and career possibilities—so that he can spend more time with his kids. What's important is that he be able to make those choices without fear that they will be used against him by his former spouse down the road. It would be patently unfair, for example, if his ex-wife demanded the same child support payments and refused to budge on the visitation schedule if her former spouse did indeed trim his work hours and take a cut in pay so that he could be around his children more often. But that sort of thing happens all the time.

Men's careers have commonly been used against them for years, but watch out when the tables get turned, as they were when famed O.J. Simpson prosecutor Marcia Clark and her estranged husband, Gordon, began battling over their two children. Marcia had asked her husband to move out of their house in December 1993, and just over a year later asked the courts for primary custody of their boys even though she was so swamped with the Simpson case that she often had to rely on a babysitter to put her children to bed at night. Devastated by her former wife's actions, Gordon filed a motion for temporary primary custody while the Simpson case was still going on, his rationale being: "Her priority is her career, mine is my children. I can be with them right now, she can't." All sound and logical thinking, right? Wrong. Gordon was ripped apart in the press and vilified as some sexist lout who wanted to penalize his former wife for having a career. But he was simply doing what he thought was best for his children. He was more available for them, and who could possibly argue that it would be better for those children to be tucked into bed each night by a nanny than by their father?

For years the courts have viewed fathers as one big repository of cash and have mandated unreasonable expenditures. In several states, for example, divorced parents can be required by courts to pay their children's college tuition. That has so irked some fathers that they challenged the legality of the practice, some successfully. Pennsylvania resident Philip Kline went to court in 1992 to terminate the child support order that required him to pay $375 a month to support his daughter, who had just turned eighteen. He believed that she had become an adult in the eyes of the law, and therefore he should not be forced to pay her college tuition or any other expenses. Shortly after Kline filed his suit, the Pennsylvania legislature passed a law making divorced parents responsible for their children's college expenses, or for at least as much as they could afford. But that did not dissuade him. In fact, he broadened his original suit to include that new law, known as Act 62, and eventually won a ruling from the state supreme court, which said that the law violated his rights and the rights of all divorced parents under the Fourteenth Amendment's equal protection clause. The justices reasoned that since parents who are still married cannot be made to pay their child's college bills, then parents who are divorced should not be subjected to such orders. By the way, Kline's daughter did attend college, and her father voluntarily paid her tuition. "I'm not big on having the government in my face, telling me what to do," he told a *New York Times* reporter.

RELOCATION

The courts have also become very involved in the issue of relocation, and since 1985, twenty-two state supreme courts have handed down rulings that were more favorable to the custodial parent who wanted to move away, even if it made it harder for the other parent to see the child. Two of the most recent to act have been California and New York. In New York, the relocating parent no longer has to prove that the move is necessary, either because of health reasons, for example, or a job transfer. The focus instead is on what is in "the best interest of the children." The court stated in its opinion that it was "unrealistic" to try and preserve the noncustodial parent's accustomed close involvement in the children's everyday life at the expense of the custodial parent's efforts to start a new life or form a new family unit. As for California, it also used to ask relocating parents to prove that the move was necessary. But now the objecting parent must demonstrate that the move will cause "substantial harm" to the children involved.

Decisions like those have made it much easier for custodial parents to move away with their children, and that has put yet another painful burden on fathers. On average they have joint or sole custody only twenty-four percent of the time, which means that the vast majority of mothers now have the right to relocate in many states whether the fathers of their children, who have legally mandated visitation rights, like it or not. And they are relocating more than ever before. Some studies indicate that seventy-five percent of mothers with custody move within four years of a separation or divorce, and that number is likely to rise in the face of so many favorable court rulings.

CHANGING TIMES FOR FATHERS

As bad as things have been for fathers, they are slowly getting better. Attitudes are changing, and men are beginning to receive some of the credit and compassion they have long deserved for being as important in a child's upbringing as a woman. "People are finally realizing that children need two parents," says an east coast social worker who has spent twenty years working with families torn apart by divorce. "There's a reason it takes two people to make a child. And that's because it's best if you have two people raising one. It makes no sense to cut out the father. It never has." Adds a veteran family court judge: "The system is beginning to understand that some fathers mother just as well as their former wives do. And I use the verb 'mother' intentionally. Many of them hear a child cry at night just as well as the mother. They are just as capable of heating bottles and changing diapers. They can provide the same sort of comfort and security."

What's fueling this new thinking on fathers? Part of it is the younger generation of judges, social workers, and attorneys that has started to make its legal presence felt when it comes to rulings on divorce and custody. They understand that the make-believe world of Ozzie and Harriet is a thing of the past and that the tasks of making money, taking care of a house, and bringing up baby today are more evenly distributed between mother and father—and that both sexes are up to the job. They have seen more mothers working nine to five outside of the home and more fathers taking care of the kids. They've seen the roles of men and women change dramatically over the years, and as a result, they don't have any problems picturing a father up to his elbows in Pampers and diaper wipes. That knowledge makes it easier for those involved in the legal process to work with the facts of a case and not be driven so much by gender prejudice. Another reason for the change is that the public at large has witnessed many of those same things, and the more they see and hear about men parenting in more complete ways, the easier it is for them as parents.

An even bigger factor, perhaps, is the trend of more and more men wanting to be with their kids. "Fathers are much more involved with their children today than they were twenty years ago," says Susan Freedland, a Greenwich, Connecticut, psychotherapist. "The phrase *joint custody* didn't even exist back then, but now you see more and more of it. And more and more fathers are asking for it, asking to be involved." A female family court jurist agrees: "We have gone from where fathers were not asserting their rights very often to a time where they are, and more people are listening," she says. "A lot of fathers didn't even try and fight in the past. Mom got custody, Dad got visitation, and that was that. Only in the most extreme cases did the father get the kids. But that's not the situation anymore. We are seeing more coparenting, more fathers getting their children, more gender-neutral thinking. You never would have seen girls living with their fathers ten years ago, but you do now."

None of this means, of course, that fathers no longer face problems. But it is safe to say that things are improving. "In the past two decades fathers have gotten at least the possibility of realizing their rights to be with their children, whether it be outright custody or visitation," says attorney Rob Skovgaard.

"But the system still works against men, and it is still not gender neutral by any stretch of the imagination."

Indeed. Talk to almost any veteran matrimonial lawyer and he or she will give you the same opinion: Fathers still face an uphill battle. One of the first things many of them do when a potential client comes to talk about fighting for custody of his children is tell him exactly what he is up against. They say that fathers seeking custody face great personal pain and expense, that they must battle imposing odds, and that they will deal with tremendous biases in favor of maternal custody no matter how good a parent they may be. They want to make sure that fathers harbor no illusions about the fight they will have to wage.

2

PREPARING FOR BATTLE

THE KEY TO WINNING ANY BATTLE IS KNOWING EXACTLY what you are up against and how best to prepare. We demonstrated in chapter 1 that men who want custody of their children are usually fighting an uphill battle simply because they are men. And that's the primary reason that they must take great pains to prepare themselves for the struggle.

FIGHTING FOR THE RIGHT REASONS

Before you begin fighting, you must examine the reasons you are willing to subject yourself–and your children–to such emotional and financial distress. Is it because you have a strong relationship with your kids and want to make sure you retain that even in the face of a messy divorce? Is it because you offer something special and unique as a parent? Is it because you were the primary caregiver during your marriage and want to continue in that role? Are there extreme circumstances such as physical abuse or drug use that call your ex-spouse's fitness as a parent into question? If you answer, "Yes" to any or all of these questions, then you are probably pursuing custody for the right reasons. But if you're looking to punish your former spouse and think a fierce battle for the children is a good way to get back at her, then you should give up all notions about becoming a custodial parent and forget about reading this book. The same is true for the man who really doesn't have that strong a desire to be a full-time parent or, for that matter, hasn't investigated what it takes to be there all the time. You shouldn't even consider fighting for your children if you're not able to work as hard at home as you do in the office, if you can't attend school functions on a regular basis, and if you're not willing to stay up half the night caring for a sick child. Parenting is something a man must want to do very badly to have even a shot at winning custody in the courts. If you feel otherwise, you would do well to save yourself some time and money and become an every-other-weekend kind of guy.

Full-time parenting is not for the faint of heart, and you need to remember that before you decide to fight for custody. You must also recognize how damaging a battle like this can be to the children involved. They will likely witness bitter arguments between you and your soon-to-be former spouse. They will sense enormous amounts of tension and anxiety. They will probably have to meet extensively with lawyers, therapists, and social workers, and might even be asked to testify in court. A custody battle is a very traumatic experience for children, and it has a lasting impact. So a father needs to make sure that his fight is important and necessary enough to put himself and his kids through that misery.

MAINTAINING THE PARENTAL RELATIONSHIP

If after considering the pros and cons of a custody battle, you still decide to fight for your children, you need to be aware of several factors. First of all, the most important things in your favor will be a solid relationship with your children and a long history of involvement as a parent. Those, more than anything else, will strengthen your case and give you at least a fighting chance. "Being there with your kids regularly is critical," says Robert Skovgaard, a Connecticut attorney who often represents children in custody cases. "I'm talking about doctor's appointments, teachers' conferences, coaching soccer teams, helping out with homework. The more integral a part of your children's life you become, the more difficult it will be for a court to take those children away from you. It is also essential with younger children, say in the two- to four-year-old range, that the father has the flexibility to spend time with them, to be there when they need him, to take care of them." Most legal experts tell fathers who try to play catch-up in the weeks before a dispute is brought to court that they have no chance. Everybody, especially the judge, will quickly see through such sudden interest as a parent.

But having a good relationship and being involved isn't always enough. You must do whatever you can to enhance your position as a strong, nurturing parent. If, for example, you begin to suspect that your marriage is doomed and a custody battle inevitable, you might want to start doing even more with your children so that you can better demonstrate to a court down the road that you are the one who should have custody. In his book, *Winning Your Divorce,* Timothy Horgan outlines a strategy intended to help a father gradually take over greater parenting responsibilities so that he may later prove he is the principal caregiver. Horgan points out that when marriages are faltering, mothers often have a tendency to drift from their families as they try to find themselves, and he argues that fathers can step into that vacuum by taking over many of the mother's domestic duties while allowing her to pursue other interests. Dad may become the one who makes dinner at home most nights, who attends the majority of the parent-teacher conferences, and who carpools regularly for the Girl Scout troop. The idea, of course, is to further build that relationship with your children and your role as a parent so that when it does come time to fight, you have a solid history of parenting and can't simply be dismissed as a disinterested Dad. You should also be able to establish a number of potential witnesses who have seen you engaging in a wide variety of activities with your children and who could speak factually about your role as a father. Timing is critical, however, and these moves must be made well enough in advance of any legal action so they will not be viewed as contrived or transparent.

Even if you aren't as prescient, there are still things you can do in the early stages of a divorce or custody battle that will help your cause. At the very least, you must maintain your involvement with your children, and you may well want to increase it. Don't do anything too conspicuous, however, because as

Horgan points out, dramatically increasing interaction with children may be perceived by the court as transparent attempts to "fool" it into thinking you are a good parent. Nevertheless, you must start thinking in the court's terms, and that means having to give *evidence* that you are a good parent. You must be able to demonstrate in court the invaluable relationship you have with your offspring. It would be a good idea to start a diary and keep track not only of things you do with your children but also of problems and concerns that crop up with your wife. But be careful not to make any entries that might prove harmful to you later on, such as recounting relationships with girlfriends or elaborating on the disdain you feel for your spouse. You never know who might have access to those writings one day. In fact, they could even become an exhibit in a court proceeding. You should also preserve pictures taken of you and your children in the past and make sure new ones are shot. Make sure you know all of your children's favorite foods, books, movies, and toys as well as their doctors, teachers, and best friends. The idea here is to show that the issue of custody really isn't an issue at all; you have been completely involved with your children from the beginning and that relationship must continue.

MOVE OUT OR WORK IT OUT?

One of the most critical issues of any failing marriage–and potential custody battle–revolves around which parent moves out of the family home and which does not. This is critical because courts are generally averse to disrupting children's lives any more than necessary in any custody case. So if the children are residing in the marital home with their mother when it comes time for a judge to make a decision, he is going to be hard pressed to uproot them from such familiar surroundings. The parent who occupies the home with the children has a tremendous edge. Therefore, if you want custody of your children, it is essential to do what you can to stay in the family home, even if it means sleeping in a guest room and setting up schedules so you and your spouse spend as little time together there as possible. For one thing, leaving the house may be construed by some legal experts as an admission that your wife is better able to care for the children or that you don't want to take care of them yourself. Also, moving out will unavoidably alter a good relationship between you and your children, and it might even do some harm; being a part-timer just isn't as good as being a father who is there every day. In addition, an opposing attorney could argue that you have abandoned your children. Even though that may be the furthest thing from the truth, the mere suggestion of that puts a man at a disadvantage.

If you do stay, it's important that you and your wife avoid any arguments or fights in front of the children while you are living out the last days of your marriage. Such arguments are bad for the parents and even worse for the kids. A court will be impressed with a father who repeatedly ducks confrontation with his estranged spouse in the best interests of the children. That's the sort of parent who will have the better chance of winning custody.

Having said that, however, there may indeed be times when a father has to pack up and leave, usually because the situation at home is so volatile that he feels he has no choice but to get out.

The best scenario under those circumstances is one in which you take your children with you. If that's not possible, find comfortable living quarters in the same general area so that the children's schools, doctors, etc., do not change when they stay with you. You can later argue persuasively before a court that such a move demonstrated the concern and sensitivity of a parent who thought mostly of his children by defusing a potentially explosive living situation and by finding a new house close to the marital home so that there was minimal disruption in their lives. If you do move out, maintain regular contact with your children. Establish a generous visitation schedule before you leave and continue your regular parenting activities with the kids once you have relocated. Organize sleepovers and parties for your children, invite your new neighbors over for family gatherings, and make your home as comfortable as possible. In other words, you should do everything you can to demonstrate that you are still a caring, capable parent.

FINDING A LAWYER

It's not unusual for married couples to find their relationships in turmoil and give serious consideration to splitting up. Many of them tumble to the edge of the abyss that is divorce, only to back off and decide to work out their differences. But a significant number of people opt to go through with the break. If you see divorce as inevitable and suspect that a custody battle is in the offing as well, you need to get a lawyer. To be sure, there are times when a lawyer might not be necessary, such as with an uncontested divorce that involves no community property or children. But otherwise, you shouldn't take any chances. You need to obtain the best representation possible, or you are going to lose your shirt–and a whole lot more.

Perhaps no decision in the entire custody process is more critical than the one you make regarding a lawyer. And because it involves the future of your relationship with your children, it may be rightfully considered one of the most important choices of your life. A good attorney can overcome a lot of judicial prejudice and make the father's dream of keeping his children a reality. A bad one can make it all disappear.

The first step is to compile a list of qualified lawyers to interview. One of the best sources of information is friends who have been through the process themselves. Solicit their thoughts on the attorneys they used as well as any advice they might have on what they learned in the process. It might also be useful for you to talk to your personal attorney–or friends who are lawyers– and ask for their recommendations. Lawyers know what makes a good lawyer, and they also have–or can quickly get–a sense of who's hot and who's not. Some legal experts say that visiting the courthouse in the judicial district in which your case will be handled is not a bad idea either. It gives you a chance to watch lawyers at work and see how they perform under fire. Local Bar associations will provide names of attorneys, as will specialty organizations such as the American Academy of Matrimonial Lawyers. Libraries also have directories that list attorneys by specialty, and if all else fails, there is always the *Yellow Pages*. But nothing can beat a personal recommendation from a trusted source.

It is wise to interview two or three attorneys before deciding on one to handle your case. Some lawyers charge a fee for the initial consultation—anywhere from $200 to $300—while others ask for nothing at all. A man should not be dissuaded from meeting with an attorney simply because he charges for an interview. One of the reasons for demanding such a fee is that by meeting with a prospective client, the attorney is effectively disqualified from representing that person's spouse. Interviews with prospective attorneys are protected by lawyer-client privilege, and all discussions are confidential. If a man shares information with an attorney about his marriage and the reasons it fell apart, that attorney would have a conflict of interest if he then talked to the man's wife. The fee serves as a sort of quid pro quo for the disqualification. Interestingly, some men have used the interviewing process as a way of neutralizing a particularly good attorney. They may have no interest in hiring a certain lawyer, either because the fees are too high or they have already found an attorney they like. But they certainly don't want their soon-to-be former wives to retain him or her, so they set up a consultation, pay the one-time fee, and walk away knowing that they have taken one powerful weapon out of their spouse's hands.

The interview will likely begin with the attorney asking the prospective client a series of questions about his personal life, his wife, his children, his marriage, the reasons it is breaking up, his finances, and other aspects of his life. The key here—and in subsequent meetings with whichever attorney you choose—is to be completely honest. A lawyer can't possibly develop a formidable defense, provide a strong sense of what a client is up against, what his chances of success are, or what his strategy may be if he doesn't have all the facts.

Next, it is the client's turn to ask questions. Following is a list of suggested queries and the responses you should expect.

1. *Do you practice matrimonial law exclusively?*

   The preferred answer is that it constitutes about eighty percent of the attorney's time. Anything less than fifty percent is not acceptable except in the most extraordinary circumstances.

2. *If not, what other areas of the law do you practice?*

   What's important here is not so much the areas themselves but that the attorney has a litigation background and can operate well in a courtroom.

3. *What is your educational background?*

   Other than for the prestige it can confer, an attorney's educational background is far less valuable than his or her experience.

4. *Do you represent both men and women?*

   It makes better sense to hire an attorney who represents men and women on an almost equal basis; that sort of background gives the lawyer a perspective into how both sides think during a divorce or custody case.

5. *Have you gone to trial?*

   Roughly ten percent of all matrimonial cases go to trial, so it is certainly helpful to have an attorney who knows how to work in court. And from a negotiating standpoint, it doesn't hurt to have the opposing lawyer be aware of your attorney's prowess in the courtroom and know that he or she is not afraid to go to trial should talks break down.

6. *What are your billing policies?*

    Attorneys are ethically mandated to provide clients with a retainer letter, and most bill on a monthly basis, which helps to keep the client apprised of the case's progress and status.

7. *Do you charge for telephone calls?*

    Most attorneys charge for telephone calls in increments of one-tenth of an hour.

8. *Do you give out your home telephone number?*

    Few attorneys do that, and the ones that do admonish their clients to use the number only in case of an emergency. A prospective client should not be put off by the fact the his lawyer does not give out his or her telephone number; it's common practice.

9. *Will you be the only attorney who works on my case, or will other lawyers in your office also participate?*

    This is a critical point. In large firms an attorney often has his associates work on a file. A client comes to a matrimonial lawyer because of his experience and background, and that's who he wants working for him. He did not hire lawyer A so that lawyers B and C could handle the case. If the attorney being interviewed says an associate, or associates, may be helping out, the prospective client has a right to expect a meeting with the associates before hiring anybody.

10. *Do you have a paralegal?*

Paralegals are helpful in the discovery phase of a case, but they are not authorized to dispense legal advice.

11. *Do your paralegals or assistants charge for their time?*

The answer should be no.

12. *What are your office hours?*

You certainly want a lawyer who is going to be available during the day and not out playing golf whenever the weather is nice. Most attorneys work from 8:30 A.M. to 6 P.M., and some have office hours on Saturday mornings.

13. *Do you consider yourself to be aggressive?*

If the case is an overly contentious one and will almost certainly end up in trial, then you need an aggressive attorney. If you are hoping to reconcile or settle amicably with your spouse, then a low-key lawyer would be more appropriate. Also, keep in mind that many judges don't have a lot of time for an overly aggressive attorney who is beating up the mother on the stand and making a lot of snide comments. A lawyer who irks the person on the bench is no help at all.

14. *If so, would you tone down your routine if asked?*

The answer should be yes.

15. *Have you ever been through the divorce process yourself?*

This is a fair question to ask a prospective attorney because it is often useful to be represented by someone who has been through the process himself. However, there is no need to delve further into his personal life.

16. *Will you reveal any of the information I give you to a third party?*

Violating attorney-client confidence is a severe breach of ethics. If the attorney answers yes or hesitates in any way, do not hire him.

17. *Do you have any opinions about whether a mother or father is a more appropriate custodial parent?*

Your attorney is working for you and you alone. Any preconceived notions must be left at the office door.

18. *Will an attorney be appointed to represent my child?*

In most contested custody cases or visitation disputes, an attorney is appointed by the court to protect the best interests of the child.

19. *Will you ever talk to my child?*

Since your child will probably have his or her own attorney during a custody dispute, the lawyers representing the parents should not speak to the child because any such contact would be unethical. The parents' attorneys should go through the child's attorney.

20. *Will you communicate with me frequently?*

An attorney should certainly return phone calls and mail his clients copies of any and all correspondence and pleadings in the case.

You should listen carefully to the answers a prospective attorney gives. Be wary of anyone who promises the world and downplays the difficulties of a custody case. Shy away from those who bad-mouth other attorneys; only people lacking in confidence and good manners behave that way, and nobody wants a lawyer who sells himself by being negative about others. It is, however, perfectly acceptable for an attorney to comment on his opponent in a case, once both lawyers have been chosen. In fact, a client would be remiss if he did not ask about the reputation and experience of his wife's lawyer. Does he like to milk cases for the legal fees? Is he reluctant to go to court? Does he have a bias against men? The matrimonial bar in most cities and counties is small, and the lawyers all know each other's strengths and weaknesses from both a negotiating and a trial perspective. Attorneys, like other professionals, have their idiosyncrasies, and a good lawyer will want to point those out to his client and discuss ways to counteract them.

It is also important to take note of what the prospective attorney does during an interview. Are there, for example, case files on the desk that bear the names of other clients? If so, the lawyer is breaching confidentiality, and there's reason to believe that he treats all his clients' materials the same way. Also, does the attorney take calls during the interview? And does he discuss other cases over the phone? Hopefully not. No one wants to pay to watch a lawyer talk to someone else, and once again he is violating attorney-client privilege by carrying on a private conversation in the presence of another person. You should expect an attorney's undivided attention during office meetings, save for an emergency. Some clients like to see family pictures on the attorney's wall or desk, and with good reason. The whole premise of a custody case is keeping a parent and his children together, and it's important to have someone who not only has a family himself but also understands the love between a parent and child. Some people feel that gender is also an important consideration when it comes to picking an attorney. Some believe, for example, that a female lawyer will better serve a man seeking custody of his children because of the pro-mother biases in many courthouses. Moves like that may have helped to some degree two decades ago, but they don't do much good in today's courtrooms where female lawyers and judges are commonplace. Besides, it's best to pick an attorney based on his or her abilities and a mutual comfort level. Selections based on gender could easily backfire.

The hunt for a good attorney may take some time, but thoroughness is often rewarded. A man should research his choices carefully. He doesn't, for example, have to limit his visit to one hour, especially if he is paying a consultation fee. He should spend two or three hours with the person if necessary, and he should feel free to schedule another appointment. As previously mentioned, observing lawyers in court is often a good way to narrow down the options. And it is a good idea to get references from previous clients.

Somewhere along the way, the interviewer needs to ask each of his prospective attorneys about their fees and billing procedures. Virtually all matrimonial lawyers require a retainer, generally ranging from $1,500 to $7,500, and charge hourly fees that run anywhere from $175 to $350. Clients are also responsible for incidental costs such as photocopying, messenger services, long-distance telephone calls, subpoena fees, etc. As a rule, the more experienced and knowledgeable the lawyer, the higher the retainer, and a New York City attorney is going to get paid more than his counterpart in Des Moines, Iowa, simply because the cost of doing business in his part of the country are higher. It is almost impossible to know in the beginning how much a case will end up costing because there are too many variables. A good attorney, however, should be able to provide a rough idea and keep a client up to date on finances by communicating regularly on the status of the case by phone and monthly billings.

Some people blanch at the cost of hiring an attorney and are tempted to go the cheapest route. But you must remember that it's your children you are fighting for, and what seems inexpensive now may end up costing you dearly in the long run. You should try and pick the attorney you feel will do the best job, not the one who is the most affordable.

THE MEDIATION OPTION

Many people, especially those put off by the extreme financial and emotional costs of a full-blown fight, consider the mediation alternative. The practice usually involves an attorney-therapist team that is retained by both parties to help them settle their custodial, visitation, and financial disputes. Frequently, the mother and father each retain their own attorneys to review the fruits of their work and give advice. In theory, the concept has a lot of merit, especially because it can save thousands of dollars if it works (the total fee will likely range from $5,000 to $10,000) and because a couple can walk away with a working relationship that will do them–and their children–much good in the years to come. There is even an organization, called the American Association for Mediated Divorce, that facilitates and encourages that approach. But mediation seems to work only when there is relatively equal bargaining power between the two parties or a genuine absence of rancor. If one of the spouses is controlling or the divorce is acrimonious, then the chances of mediation succeeding are remote. Still, it is an option worth exploring, for anything that lessens the conflicts that arise with divorces and custody battles, especially for the kids, is welcome.

BRACING THE CHILDREN

While you are shopping for an attorney and thinking about the option of mediation, you must also perform perhaps the most difficult task of all–telling your children about the custody battle and all it will entail. You should tell them in a timely fashion, preferably with your wife. Even children as young as four should be told. Children that age will learn about the family's problems eventually and any attempt to hide the truth will only heighten their anxiety and stress. Finding out about their parents' impending divorce or custody battle from classmates at school or neighborhood friends will only make things harder. As Dr. Stephen Herman explains in his book, *Parent vs. Parent– How You and Your Child Can Survive the Custody Battle,* the father and mother don't have to go into great detail when they discuss the situation with their younger children, but they do need to make them aware of what is going on. Among other things, it validates the children's own feelings and perceptions and allows them to trust their judgment. If they see Mommy and Daddy fighting, but the parents keep telling the children that everything is all right, they will become confused and even more anxious about the situation.

How a parent breaks the news depends on the child's age; the older the child, the more information he will likely want and the more intense his reaction might be. Whatever the age, it's important that the children be told in no uncertain terms that their mother and father love them very much, that they will always love them, that they will be there to take care of them, and that the children had nothing to do with the divorce or custody dispute. Some therapists believe it is best not to tell children on a school night, suggesting a weekend day instead so that the kids will have some time to digest the information and talk about it with their mother and father.

Herman cautions parents against leaning too heavily on older children during such difficult times and treating them more as friends than as sons or daughters. Having to act as one parent's confidant, to hear complaints about the other parent, or to pick sides is a terribly unfair burden for a young boy or girl and it only makes it harder to deal with an already difficult situation.

DOS AND DON'TS

Now that you have selected your attorney and told your children, you are ready to start building your case and planning your strategy. But as you ready yourself for the battle ahead, you need to be aware of some simple dos and don'ts:

1. *Be cool.* Few things are as emotionally charged as a custody dispute, but it is important not to let those emotions get the best of you. You must think before you act. You

should talk to your attorney before you respond to any provocative action your spouse might have taken. You shouldn't leave nasty phone messages or nasty notes. You shouldn't go over to your wife's home if you know the visit is only going to lead to confrontation. And no matter how frustrated you might be, you must not bad-mouth your spouse in front of your children. You may absolutely hate her at certain points in the process and want to scream about the horrible way she is treating you. That's fine; don't just do it in front of the kids. You should never let them see the degree of your disdain for her.

2. *Don't move in with your lover.* In fact, you might even want to consider putting the relationship on hold for the time being. Technically, you are still married, and even though dating during your separation is hardly immoral, you can never be too sure how a judge might react to it. If you do continue to date, you shouldn't introduce your lover to your children until after the case is settled or tried.

3. *Forget the babysitter for a while.* You should spend time with your children when you have them and shelve your social life for a while. It won't be easy convincing a judge that you should have custody if you are shuffling the kids off to a babysitter or relatives all the time.

4. *Behave.* You should obey the law, not drink a lot, not drive after you have been drinking, not drive recklessly, or do anything that will land your name in the police

blotter section of the local newspaper. Any brushes with the law will be used against you, and they certainly won't help your chances.

5. *Be careful in any dealings with the wife.* There's a reason why the two of you have hired lawyers and are trying to settle your differences in court: you don't get along and probably haven't for some time. If your relationship has been historically unequal or if there is an enormous amount of animosity, forget about dealing with each other individually and work through your lawyers. But if there are some issues that they can resolve together, then by all means give it a try. It will lessen the acrimony in court and keep legal costs down. But you should approach this area cautiously; divorce and custody battles often bring out the worst in people, and there's no telling when one of the parties will blow up.

6. *Be careful with your therapist.* Therapy is often a tremendously helpful outlet for people struggling through a divorce or custody battle. It enables them to deal honestly with important emotional issues and regain a sense of confidence and self-worth at a time when everything around them seems to be falling apart. The process is also helpful in alleviating conflict between two people, mainly because it frequently forces them to focus on what they as individuals can do to make things better and not on blaming or punishing the other person. We would encourage men and women in the midst of a divorce or custody fight to consider therapy, but we must

also raise a note of caution: In some states a judge can force a therapist to waive the confidentiality privilege and testify in court if he feels that it is important to know more about a plaintiff's or defendant's psychological make-up. Check with your lawyer about the rules governing that issue in your state.

Another point on the subject: some older judges still find going to a therapist somewhat aberrant behavior. But the younger generation on the bench has no problem with it.

7. *What about therapy for the children?* This is an issue for the parents to decide together, perhaps with some input from their pediatrician. Again, therapy can be a useful option for children caught in the turmoil of divorce and custody battles and should definitely be considered. If a child does go to a therapist, it should not be the same one as either of the parents. The fear there is that the therapist would have some preconceived notions and might not be as objective in his work.

8. *Forget about guilt.* You must not let that emotion get the better of you or your judgment. You may feel bad because you have ended a marriage. You may feel guilty about the pain your wife and children are feeling. You may feel terrible about wanting the kids to live with you and how that wish is tearing up your family. You may feel so bad that you start giving away the store in a time of emotional weakness. Your wife can have the house. She can have most of the money. She can have the kids.

Don't do it. The vast majority of marriages fall apart as a result of the actions of both parties, and no one person can or should be blamed. You should never let emotions dictate what you decide to do in your divorce or custody battle. If you truly want your children and think that having custody is in their best interests, then you cannot let guilt make you act otherwise.

We know a man who was separated and met a woman about the same time he was working out a divorce agreement with his wife. He was very excited about the possibilities of this new relationship and talked to several friends about it. He also mentioned it to his therapist, who quickly asked: "Have you slept with her yet?" Our friend said no, and the therapist advised not to until everything was settled with his wife. "I don't want you walking into your lawyer's conference room the day after you've made love to that woman, see your wife, begin feeling bad about getting involved with another woman, and then start giving your wife more money, possessions, and even custody of your children just because you feel guilty." It was excellent advice. Our friend waited, got most of what he wanted in his divorce agreement and then started what turned out to be a wonderful new relationship.

9. *Learn to cook.* It's important if you want to gain custody of your kids that the court knows you can prepare a wholesome meal and don't have to rely entirely on fast food. If you don't know how to cook by the time legal proceedings begin, you should learn, and learn fast.

Also, you should make sure that your refrigerator is well-stocked whenever you have your kids. Social workers and attorneys representing children often make it a point when they visit a family's home for an interview of asking for something to drink just so they can see what's inside the fridge.

10. *Quit smoking.* A no-brainer. Smoking does come up as an issue in custody fights, and the father who smokes should give it up right away. It'll help your case in court as well as your health. And it might even give you a lot more years with your children.

3

ONCE YOU HAVE PREPARED YOURSELF FOR BATTLE, IT'S TIME for the legal proceedings to begin. The big question is Who should bring the action? Sometimes you have no choice in the matter because a sheriff has already appeared at your front door with papers informing you that your wife is filing for divorce or moving to modify the existing custody arrangement. But if that hasn't yet happened, you should be prepared to make the first move.

INITIATING LEGAL ACTION

In years past most lawyers thought it preferable for the man to let the woman bring the action. The thinking was that if he made the motion, the judge would assume that he was the one giving up on the marriage and might be more inclined to see the wife as an innocent victim. Let her file, the rationale went. That way, she looked more like the instigator, the one who was leaving, and perhaps the judge would not be so quick to give her everything she wanted. In addition, some parents were reluctant to bring the action because they were afraid their children would view them as the ones who asked for the divorce.

Those concerns are all valid, but they do nothing to change our belief that, these days, it's better for the man to initiate the legal proceedings. By doing so, he gets to tell his story first in court, and judges say that can have a big impact on their opinion. It allows a father to build a strong case about his attributes as a parent and, at the same time, plant some subtle seeds of doubt about the mother's capabilities. The mother will eventually be able to tell her side of the story, but it will be hard for the judge not to consider what her husband has just said and wonder whether the woman is telling the truth.

SETTING GOALS AND PRIORITIES

However the action is brought, when it finally happens it means that the legal ball is rolling. That's a good time for you to review what your goals are in this battle, what you must do to accomplish them, and how you should handle yourself during what is sure to be an emotionally and financially taxing process. The most important thing is remaining focused on the children and what is best for them. Every decision, every tactic, every move must be weighed on how it will affect the kids in both the long and short term. You may be so angry at your wife that you want to destroy her in every way. You may want to scream at her whenever your paths cross and deny her even the most basic allowances of child support and alimony. You may want to see her ravaged on the stand by your lawyer and humiliated in the community. But what good does any of that bring the children? The woman is, after all, their mother, and unless she is an extraordinarily troubled soul, she will be a part of their lives for as long as she lives. It's important, then, that she remain a strong and confident person, that she have some semblance of self-esteem, and that she be the sort of person her children can love and respect. Destroying her could destroy their chance at a solid relationship with their mother, which is critical whether the parents are divorced or not. It could also ruin their image of her, which would be extremely harmful to the children's development. And it certainly won't help your relationship with the mother of your children once the fight is over if you spend most of your time trying to beat her brains out legally.

You need to remember that no matter what happens, you and your wife are going to have to continue dealing with each other for a good many years, and the sooner you start to develop a workable and reasonable postmarital relationship, the better. It will make things easier for you, to be sure. But even more importantly, it will help out the children, who won't have such a hard time dealing with the trauma of a divorce and custody battle if Mom and Dad are able to handle it all like mature adults. Granted, it won't always be easy to rise above the inevitable slights and barbs that come with a legal battle. Things that were said in love will be used as battering rams, and the impulse to respond in kind will be strong. The key is for you to remember that you are battling for what is best for your kids. You should fight to win, but not at any cost.

The second most important thing you must do is formulate a winning strategy with your attorney and be ready to implement it immediately when the proceedings start. Remember that, as a man, you begin the process at a distinct disadvantage. But you can overcome all that if you are able to present a case that demonstrates you are the better parent, that you are the one most available for your children, that you are the inevitable choice. "Men in this situation need to sell themselves on why they are better, to show why and how they are indispensable parts of their children's lives, to highlight all their positives," says attorney Robert Skovgaard. "But they must do so in a way that doesn't bash their wives at the same time. It would be better for you to say, 'I do A, B, C with my children while my wife does X, Y, Z, and here's why A, B, C is better." Instead of saying, for example, that your wife never takes the children to their soccer games and horseback riding lessons on the weekends, you should simply point out that you is the one who takes care of those tasks. You should describe all that you do with your children, whether it's cooking breakfast or taking them to the doctor or attending school conferences, and do so in a way that shows consideration for the kids and minimal contempt for the mother.

THE TIME FRAME FOR CUSTODY CASES

It's almost impossible to predict how each custody case is going to unfold, for there are any number of variables that can unexpectedly slow the process down or speed it up. But we can lay out a general time line that gives a sense of how things might proceed with a custody battle that is part of an ongoing divorce, as well as one that occurs when one party moves to modify an existing arrangement or relocate after a divorce has been finalized. Keep in mind when reading this section that settlements may be reached at any time from the serving of papers right up to the day the judge is set to hand down his decision. And in the vast majority of cases, you are much better off if you can work out an agreement with an estranged spouse than if you let a complete stranger decide what should happen with your children.

Once papers are served in a divorce, it takes up to three weeks for the lawyers representing the two parties to get fully retained and begin talking. They'll need at least one week after that to figure out whether they might have a custody battle on their hands. If that's the case, the two sides can start to work out a temporary custody arrangement. If that's not possible, they will go before a judge to argue their cases and seek an order on where the children will live while the divorce is completed. Either one of those procedures could take another two weeks.

Temporary custody issues only become relevant when a man and woman separate and begin residing in different homes. Though it sounds innocuous enough, there is rarely anything good about having a judge decide temporary custody, and such a situation should be avoided at all costs. For one thing, a court intervention like that would probably take place at what is called a motion calendar proceeding before a judge who might be dealing with thirty to forty cases that particular day. The most time a temporary custody hearing might be given under those circumstances is three hours, hardly enough for a complicated custody case. And it would come only six weeks or so after papers have been served, well before the father has adequately prepared a strategy, defense, or witnesses. You can't possibly have enough time in that scenario to present a full picture of why you are the preferable parent, and if you lose at that hearing and are denied custody or given diminished visitation rights, then it will be hard to change that ruling down the road, even with a different judge. They are, after all, members of the same court and are loathe to alter each other's rulings.

For all those reasons, it is advised that you not leave the marital home and continue to cohabitate with your wife until the divorce is final, even if it pains you to be around her. Because temporary custody is not an issue if both parents are living under the same roof, a ruling on where the children should reside during the divorce proceedings is unnecessary. If staying together simply isn't possible, you should try and work out some sort of custodial solution with your spouse outside the court. If you are successful at that, the two sides would then craft a letter of agreement spelling out the provisions of the deal. That pact would be binding during the legal proceedings but would have no bearing on a future trial. In other words, if you negotiate a temporary arrangement that gives you only two days a week with your children and the mother five, the fact that you have a smaller percentage of time with your kids could not be used against you during the trial. Working out an agreement like that won't be easy for either of you, especially if your relationship has become acrimonious, but considering the alternatives, it's important to try.

If the parties have not been able to reach a custody agreement on their own, the court will appoint an attorney for the children and in many states refer the case to a state-run division known as Family Relations, which is often asked to examine the facts of a custody case and make recommendations to the court. (We'll discuss this in greater detail later on.) Generally, it will take Family Relations anywhere from four to seven months to complete their study. Once that's done, the parties will apply for a court date and should learn within the next two weeks when they will all meet before a judge and who that judge will be. Usually that's another two or three months down the road. The trial itself will last anywhere from five to eight days, and it might take the judge approximately four to six weeks to render a decision. That will likely be twelve to fourteen months from the day papers were first filed. There is next a twenty- to thirty-day appeal period. If one of the parties initiates an appeal, it could take as long as nine months for that process to run itself out.

The time frame for a postjudgment modification (when one party wants to change an existing custody agreement) or a relocation (when one party wants to move away with the minor children) is somewhat different. These scenarios, too, often start with the filing and serving of papers by the parent who wants to alter the arrangement. In the case of a relocation, the first step for a parent trying to stop that move is to file for a restraining order keeping the children in town or to force the other parent to bring the children back if they already have left. Once that is done, the case proceeds more or less as we have described above. The time needed for a Family Relations study may not be as great if one was done during the divorce proceedings and is

only a few years old. The same is true with a postjudgment
modification; once papers are filed, the process begins—and is
carried out—in much the same way.

The courts may react differently to the various types of custody cases, but you can expect one thing to remain constant:
The system is horribly overburdened. Calendars are crowded,
judges are stretched to the limit, and Family Relations is
swamped. And all that can make a tough situation even more
difficult.

DEALING WITH CHILDREN
DURING THE BATTLE

There are several things you need to keep in mind with regard
to your children as the custody battle heats up, including the following dos and don'ts:

1. Keep the children out of it. "It's very important not to put
   children in the middle of any dispute," says therapist
   Susan Freedland. "Some parents are very subtle about
   getting their kids involved, and some are not. The important thing is not to do it at all. Don't give messages to the
   other parent through your children. Don't hand them the
   child-support check. Don't put down the other parent in
   their presence. Don't cross-examine them after a visit."

2. Treat children age-appropriately. "Parents need to be
   sensitive to the developmental stages of their children as
   they go through a divorce or custody dispute," says Dr.
   Stephen Herman. "Being honest with the children in an
   age-appropriate way is the best policy. A child as young

as three can be told that Mommy and Daddy can't agree on where she should live, and that they will try and work it out with a judge. It is wrong to tell the children that Mommy and Daddy are fighting over them." Herman is also quick to point out, as are many other experts, that children should never be asked to testify in a custody case. "You don't have to be a board-certified psychiatrist to imagine the trauma that would create," he says. We agree that children should never testify, no matter their age or the nature of the dispute. There may be extraordinary circumstances where it's appropriate for a judge to hear from a child in chambers with lawyers and a court reporter present, perhaps in one involving allegations of sexual abuse. But those would be very rare.

3. Be aware that everything that happens with the children will be scrutinized during the proceedings. Remember that scene in *Kramer* vs. *Kramer* when the boy fell off the jungle gym on the playground? Things like that still matter, and you should be extra careful, never leaving the children alone or unsupervised.

4. Do not discuss any new romantic interests with your children or bring them along on dates. It's far too confusing for them and can only reflect badly on you if brought up in court.

5. You should be flexible with respect to visitation arrangements, including pick-ups and drop-offs.

6. Don't eavesdrop on telephone conversations with the other parent.

7.   Try to keep copies of any or all school papers or pictures of the kids that might one day be helpful in court. For example, keep a drawing by your child that shows the two of you together and leaves the mother out or puts her in a distant corner. Be sure to note the date for reference.

8.   Make sure your children understand that they are not the cause of the marriage break-up or the custody battle. The problems are a result of Mommy and Daddy not being able to get along. Assure the children that both parents love them and will always be there for them.

9.   If you can only remember one thing, it must be this: In every instance, consider the best interests of the children first.

Legal Counsel for the Children

If the parents in a custody battle are unable to reach an agreement early in the process and a trial seems probable, or if the case involves relocation or a change in visitation, the court will likely appoint a lawyer for the minor children involved. Often, the request for that counsel, who must be paid by the parents, is made by either the father or mother and their attorneys, though a judge may act on his own if he believes it is in the best interest of the children. The idea is to have someone, usually a local attorney who is known to the court as well as the parents' lawyers, to represent the children's needs and desires and make sure their voices are heard. If such an attorney is retained, he will likely have a significant impact on the judge's thinking and will therefore play a critical role in the case. For that reason, you and your lawyer should try to work with the mother and her counsel on selecting a suitable attorney for the children. In this way, you will have some control of the pick and might even be able to secure an attorney sympathetic to a father's position. Otherwise, you will be putting the choice entirely in the judge's hands, breaking one of the most important rules of custody battles: Don't give other people the power to make decisions over your children.

The attorney representing children who have intelligence and maturity enough to express their feelings–usually those over the age of six–has a markedly different role than the lawyer retained for kids who are younger. The lawyer for the older children will work with them much as he does with his other clients, listening carefully to their desires and then trying to get them what they want. The attorney who tends to the younger kids is known as a "guardian ad litem" and has the delicate job of speaking on their behalf and deciding after a careful consideration of the facts–and without any real verbal feedback from his clients–what is best for them. There is no hard-and-fast rule as to when a court will start listening to children who are well-spoken and able to say what they want; it all depends on their maturity and emotional stability. Generally, if a twelve-year-old who is a good student and appears to be well-adjusted says he wants to live with his father, and his father is a good dad, the judge will almost certainly grant his request.

THERAPISTS FOR THE CHILDREN

The court will sometimes appoint therapists for children. Their goal is to ferret out the real from the imagined with the kids, to help see the stresses and frustrations caused by the divorce and custody process, and to recognize symptoms of depression, post-traumatic stress disorder, tension, and anxiety. They can also help detect when "brainwashing" has taken place and prove or disprove claims of physical or sexual abuse. In addition, therapists, who must also be reimbursed by the parents, give the court an opportunity to hear from a neutral party who can provide an important perspective on the children's emotional states.

For that reason, we think the appointment of therapists is a good idea if it's necessary and the therapist is capable. But keep in mind that there is no firm set of qualifications an expert witness must have. Therefore, it's important for a father to be very involved in the selection of potential evaluator. You need a mental health professional who is trained to deal with children. You also want one who lives nearby and is able to meet easily and regularly with all parties. You should know where the therapist went to school, where he practices, and whether he is affiliated with a teaching or clinical institution.

Once an evaluator has been chosen and then completed his study, he will make his report known not only to the judge but also to the parents and their attorneys. You should listen carefully to your findings and see if they present an opportunity to settle the case before it goes any further. If you are dissatisfied with the report of the initial therapist, you can get another expert to review the study and point out its flaws. But that, too, will cost some money; expert witnesses, even when appointed by the judge, are not cheap.

PREPARING YOUR CASE

After you have considered your children, you then need to take care of yourself. For one thing, you should keep a private diary of all that goes on, not only with your children but also with your soon-to-be ex-wife. You should record comments your kids make voluntarily about their mother, whether it has to do with her boyfriend, her lifestyle, anything that might have some bearing on the case. You should keep track of statements your wife makes about herself, her job, her children. Perhaps she is extremely stressed by the whole process and confides that she is feeling depressed. Maybe she finds the life of a working single parent taxing and complains of having a hard time working and caring for the kids at the same time. Information such as that can help a man's case, and you should keep your ears open and pen ready throughout the process. You would also be smart to send copies of all entries to your lawyer; as part of attorney-client correspondence, their confidentiality would be protected from any attempts by the opposition to gain access to them.

It would also be helpful to provide your attorney with an account of your married life that is as complete as possible, highlighting the most critical moments. Was there a lot of drinking? Drug abuse? Infidelity? Fights? Were there any emotional breakdowns? Was your wife able to hold down a good job? Was she able to take care of herself financially? Did she spend recklessly? What sort of personal secrets did she share with you?

What was her family like? Her friends? How did she act with the children? How did that change, if at all, over the years? What caused the marriage to fall apart? The more information you give your attorney, the better prepared you both will be at the negotiating table and in the courthouse. Perhaps none of it will be used—and you have to be clear with your lawyer on exactly what you want introduced into the case. But even if information is not introduced, it will still give the attorney a better sense of who his client's spouse is and what she is all about. It will help him decide what tactics to employ not only in court but also in negotiations. And it will give you material that might prove very useful if things get ugly.

This is also a good time for you to consider talking with the mother of your children about the possibility of settling the custody case out of court. Obviously, the subject will have been broached before, but it is not a bad idea to bring up the idea again if there's a chance that talks might work. Under no circumstances should you cut a deal with your wife without the assistance of a lawyer. But it is fine for you to lay the groundwork for such a pact if the two parties are of relatively equal bargaining power; you just need to make sure that your lawyer looks at anything you are thinking of signing. Even if you can't reach total agreement, you can still accomplish a lot by working out issues such as schooling, religious education, insurance plans, etc. It will save you money you would have otherwise spent on attorneys and time in court. It will create less acrimony in the custody case and smooth the way for better parental relations in the future. And it will ease the emotional burden for the children if they see Mommy and Daddy working together. If the parties are not operating from equal bargaining positions, then they are better off having their attorneys do the talking.

YOUR DAY IN COURT

Even while you are talking settlement, you would do well to begin preparing yourself for trial. One of the most difficult parts of that process is taking the stand. Here are some tips on being the best possible witness:

1. Be prepared. You should spend plenty of time working with your lawyer so you feel comfortable when you step into the courtroom. In fact, it's a good idea to have your attorney take you to the actual courtroom in which the case will be tried and question you there when it's empty so you know how it will feel. Atmosphere is important.

2. Carefully review all depositions and prior court transcripts involving the case. Don't let trial testimony be inconsistent with what's been stated in the deposition. That will hurt because credibility is important with a judge. Remember, divorce and custody cases are heard before judges, not juries.

3. You should be sure your lawyer conducts a thorough mock cross-examination in the same manner as the opposing attorney. Perhaps, you could engage the services of another attorney in the office to handle the mock cross-examination, preferably an attorney of the same sex as the attorney representing the mother.

4. At all times, answer only the question asked of you by the

opposing attorney and never volunteer any information. If the question calls for a yes or no response, then answer yes or no.

5. Don't answer any question you don't understand; if necessary, ask for help of the judge at trial.

6. Make some eye contact with the judge during the proceeding, and don't be afraid to show emotion if the situation warrants it. But don't be phony.

WITNESSES

As you get yourself ready to take the stand, you might also want to start thinking of people who could attest to your abilities as a parent, either by writing the court on your behalf or testifying themselves. It is best to come up with a group of three "fact witnesses," perhaps a school teacher, a day-care provider and a doctor, who have seen you with your children and can support your claims of being an active, available, and involved parent. These people must refrain from commenting on broader issues of the case and making sweeping statements about your abilities as a parent. Rather, they should give just the facts. The teacher, for example, could tell the court that it was you who brought your children to school most of the time, who came in to read to the class once a week, and who attended all of the parent-teacher conferences. But there shouldn't be any comments on whether you are a better parent or on where the child would be happiest living. The teacher isn't qualified to make those sorts of judgments, and the opposing attorney would tear her to pieces on the stand if she did. This is also true with a doctor, who should only comment on the fact that it was you who brought the child into most of his appointments, and the day-care provider, who saw you drop off and pick up the children from the center ninety percent of the time.

It is also appropriate in a custody case to bring in a couple of character witnesses, friends or neighbors who can shed more personal light on your devotion to your children and the way you take care of them. Their testimony, however, will likely be discounted to a certain degree by the judge. "These people are his friends," he will think to himself. "I expect them to say something good." Still, their words of praise won't hurt, so long as they follow the advice outlined above: Stick to the facts, keep focused on the qualities of the father and not the faults of the mother, and avoid making general assertions they can't really back up.

Often, people are tempted to call their therapist–or their children's therapist–to the witness stand. Forget about it. Your visits with your shrink, and those of your kids, are supposed to be private. Making them a part of a custody battle upsets that. The normal rules of patient-therapist confidentiality are waived during testimony, and a great deal of damage can be done to the doctor-patient relationship if it does not go well in court. You would be wise not to let your or your children's therapist get directly involved in the case, either by writing letters to the court or testifying. If you or your lawyer want to present a psychological evaluation, you should hire an outside expert instead.

MEETING WITH YOUR EVALUATORS

You also need to prepare yourself for visits with people from the Family Relations division and other court evaluators, including the children's attorney. The first meetings will take place on a one-on-one basis, and it's important that you remember to emphasize your positives and not your wife's negatives. Perhaps you should open up the conversation by talking about your experiences with your children and why you are seeking primary physical custody or more expanded visitation, or why you are trying to prevent the mother from moving out of state. You should be as thoughtful and even-tempered as possible. It's fine if you express your frustration with having to fight for custody of the children and how it pains you. But you should not rant and rave about the unfairness of the situation and how badly your wife is treating you. The evaluators want to see a person who is under control and can get over all the emotional agony of a divorce and custody battle well enough to raise his children in a proper way, not someone who seems on the verge of falling apart.

When it comes time for the evaluators to meet with both you and the children, you should make the situation and atmosphere as comfortable as possible. Make sure the house is tidy, but don't go overboard and have it steam-cleaned. That may look a little too neurotic to some social workers and might cause concern about how compulsive Dad could be in other ways with the kids. As mentioned in chapter 2, it helps to have a well-stocked refrigerator because the evaluator is likely to ask for something to drink just to see if there's something other than beer and frozen pizza inside. In addition, evaluators often go up to look at a child's room. "I don't need to see a computer for the kids," says attorney Robert Skovgaard. "But I like to know that the children have a place that is their own room, that looks and feels like it is their own."

As for parents speaking ill of each other, Skovgaard says he expects it in most cases and doesn't let it bother him if it's mild. "But I get worried about the mean-spirited stuff I might hear during the one-on-one meetings," he says. "And I get even more worried if it comes out while the kids are there. That to me could be an indication that the parent is not the best. He or she should know better than to do that in front of the kids, and it gets me thinking that maybe the children's needs would best be met by not being with that parent." Skovgaard says he also looks a lot at patterns in trying to anticipate what the future holds. "If one parent has held the same job for a few years and lived in the same house while the other one has moved around a lot, I might be concerned about what would happen to the children if the more transient parent had custody," he explains.

OTHER ISSUES

There are several other things you should be prepared to deal with during the early stages of a custody fight:

1. *Firing your attorney.* Sometimes, in spite of all your hard work in finding the best possible lawyer, you simply make a mistake in your selection and start to become dissatisfied with the work of your counsel. Perhaps the attorney is not returning phone calls or doesn't keep you informed of all court motions and procedures. You may

even hear from your wife that her attorney is having trouble getting in touch with your lawyer as well. If any or all of the above are the case, you would do well to cut your losses and find better representation. But you must make sure you are not putting all the blame for an overburdened legal system and a difficult case on your attorney's shoulders. Every litigant, it seems, has a story of how a brother, uncle, cousin, or nephew fared better in a custody case. They lose patience, and then they lash out at their lawyer by firing him. Some people get so frustrated that they go through three or four attorneys in a case, which won't help them out in court. Judges are human beings, and when they see a series of attorneys representing a client, they sometimes view it as a sign of instability as a client. And that could translate in their minds into instability as a parent.

2. *Judge shopping.* In many jurisdictions, judges rotate on a six-month or yearly basis. Certain members of the bench are more pro-father than others, and a good lawyer can help plan your case from a timing and filing perspective around the more favorable judge.

3. *What if your wife tries to force you to move out?* Women have been known to go to extraordinary lengths to get you to move out of the marital home, even if the couple has previously agreed to live there until the divorce and custody battle are over. You should do what you can to stay in the house. If your wife starts to get nasty, you must avoid confrontation with her at all costs. You

should never threaten violence and certainly never assault or hit her, no matter how much she may provoke. If she hits you, you should walk away. Some attorneys advise a man who has been drinking not to go home to a potentially explosive situation; stay with a friend and return the following day. Others say that if you sense trouble, you should bring a witness with you or use a tape recorder to record troublesome conversation. If the woman continues to say she cannot stand to live in the same house with you, you should offer to finance her relocation and provide a generous support arrangement; not only will that defuse the domestic conflict but it will also leave you with the advantage when the case is finally heard.

4. *Keeping sane.* Few things can eat at you like a divorce or custody battle, so you must take good care of yourself throughout the process. You should eat well, get plenty of rest, exercise regularly, pursue your favorite pastimes whenever possible, take the occasional vacation, spend extra time with your children, and lean a little bit on your friends. You should do whatever puts some extra pleasure into your life and relieves some of the emotional burden. Watch out for excessive drinking or any drug abuse; they won't solve a thing and can only cause problems down the road.

4

Custody and Settlement Variations

Everybody rose when Judge Joseph Steinberg strode into his courtroom. A bearded father of two and grandfather of four who has been married for more than forty years, he eased into his seat, put on his reading glasses, and began to speak. "I am the presiding judge of Connecticut's statewide custody court," he said in a tone that was both stern and solicitous. "And I want to talk about your responsibilities here today." Steinberg looked squarely at the two litigants before him, the mother and father, as he uttered those words.

"The focus today is on your children and what is best for them," he explained. "If you recognize that, this case will settle, and you will have a voice. If not, we will go to trial, and I will make all the decisions. I'm a good judge, but you know better than I what is best for your children. You would never consider asking me to decide what foods you should eat or clothes you should wear. How then could you possibly let me decide what is best for your children?"

Judge Steinberg paused as he took off his glasses. "Normally, a courthouse is a battlefield, a place where lawyers go to war," he said. "The emphasis is on winning. The lawyers are warriors, and the tone is combat. But not today. Today, you two parents are in the spotlight, and the emphasis is on settlement. I expect the two of you to take responsibility for settling this case, to offer solutions for your children, solutions you know are fair.

"A custody trial is a terribly degrading and demeaning experience," he continued. "You will hear and say things that leave scars. The process will cost you the equivalent of a college education for one of your children. And it will damage them. But today, you have one last chance to avoid all that."

So began another morning in Judge Steinberg's courtroom, where only Connecticut's most difficult and seemingly hopeless custody battles ended up. Recently retired, he gave this speech every time he sat before a mother and father fighting for their children, and then he gave them the rest of the day to try one last time to settle before going to trial. Usually, the deck seemed stacked against the judge because every other attempt to resolve these cases had failed, but he rang up a remarkable record: Of the 215 disputes that came before him in 1995 and 1996, for example, all but thirty-five settled. There were several reasons for that stunning rate of success, including Steinberg's development of an innovative mediation program that has lawyers and therapists working together on cases as teams. But a large part of his success was also due to the thoughtful talk he gave the parents that appear before him. Nothing we have ever read or heard captures so well the essence of why fathers and mothers in custody cases must try to settle their differences on their own. And it is hard to understand how anybody who truly cares about their kids cannot be moved by Judge Steinberg's words and become more inclined to work out a reasonable agreement.

JOINT CUSTODY

Settlement is the desired result of any custody battle, as long as it takes into account the best interests of the children and also the needs and desires of the parents who want to care for them. Not surprisingly, it can take many forms. The most common these days is joint custody, which gives both parents equal input into all major decisions affecting the health, education, and welfare of their children. There are several variations of that alternative. One is joint physical custody, in which the children actually divide time equally with Mom and Dad. It might be one week with the father and then one with the mother, both of whom must live in the same general area for this to have any chance of working. Or it could be broken up into fortnights, with one dinner or overnight with the other parent set up during each two-week period. Whatever the split, most therapists think there are better ways to go. Although arrangements like those might be good for parents because neither one has to "give up" custody, they could well hurt the children in the long run because they deprive them of a primary home and force them to constantly change houses. "It's a dreadful situation, especially for children who are of school age," says one east coast social worker with more than 20 years of experience handling divorce and custody cases. "Very rarely can the parents and children handle that sort of relationship well."

Another option is joint custody with expanded visitation, which calls for the children to live primarily with one parent but gives the other, for example, three weekends a month with the kids, a sleepover every Wednesday night, every weekend with a Monday holiday (Memorial Day, Labor Day, etc.), and half the summer. That's probably easier on the children than joint physical, though it still moves them around a lot. Other joint custody agreements may designate one parent as the primary caregiver and give the other a more traditional visitation schedule of every other weekend, every other holiday, and perhaps one month in the summer. Although that doesn't allow the noncustodial parent as much time with the children as the other two scenarios, it does provide the children with the stability of one primary home and a less frenetic visitation routine.

Joint custody often means that the children have two fully appointed bedrooms and two sets of toys, books, clothes, etc. This may be confusing at times, but the arrangement does have its advantages. It give the kids the opportunity to do homework with both of their parents throughout the school year, for example, and allows both parents to put them to bed on a regular basis. In short, it allows both Mom and Dad to be actively involved in their children's lives. Another plus is that joint custody can work for parents who live just around the corner from each other as well as for those residing three thousand miles apart, though there would obviously be no weekend visitation in the latter case. To be sure, joint custody requires a remarkable amount of cooperation on the part of the parents, and for it to work well, there must be great flexibility. Vacation plans may need to be altered and other unanticipated changes often come up. In addition, special attention must always be paid to what is best for the children so they are not bound to schedules and routines that suit their parents' needs more than they suit their own.

OTHER ALTERNATIVES

Fathers and mothers, it seems, are always looking for new and different ways to deal with their children after a divorce, and one of the more unusual developments in recent years has been dubbed "birdnesting." It calls for the father and mother to split the marital home after the divorce, letting the children stay there full time and having the parents move in and out, perhaps on a weekly or biweekly basis. Not surprisingly, this is a highly controversial alternative, but it can conceivably work if there is a maximum level of cooperation and communication between the parties involved. Initial reports show that some children have reacted favorably to this sort of set-up, but it is so new and untested that its long-term viability, especially as it relates to the best interests of the kids, is not easy to determine.

Yet another alternative is vesting sole custody in one parent, but that's not necessarily always in the best interests of the children either. In this scenario, all decision-making authority is put in the hands of one parent, and he or she has complete control over what the children do—from the places they go to school to the religion they practice—while their former spouse gets only modest visitation. It's rarely good to isolate a father or mother so completely, and we hate to see it happen except when one parent is clearly unfit or completely disinterested. Children need both a father and mother, and the more equal and cooperative the arrangement between the parents, the better for all involved.

SIBLINGS

Many times in a divorce and custody fight, children from the same marriage will express preferences to live with different parents. Although there is no black-letter rule of law indicating that siblings should be kept together, it is rare for a court to split them up. The prevailing wisdom is that siblings belong together, especially during an emotionally traumatic time, and that they provide a strong and important support network for each other. When siblings are separated, it's usually because of extraordinary circumstances. We know of a case where a fifteen-year-old boy clearly bonded more with his father, while his three-year-old sister enjoyed a much closer relationship with her mother. The brother and sister had little in common and rarely played together, so the court decided to let them live in different homes, although it did insist that they did spend at least two visitation weekends together a month with their respective parents. Says a veteran social worker: "Every family is unique, and it is very hard to generalize. But I feel that the younger the children, the greater the disservice it is to them not to allow them the chance to grow up with siblings. But when you have a case of a parent who cannot handle two children at the same time, for example, or one like the two kids who were a dozen years apart in age, then you might have to make adjustments."

The types of custody are many, but whatever arrangement is reached, it should always allow for frequent telephone contact between the children and the parents. We think that one telephone call a day, perhaps before bed, is important for both children and the absent parent. The calls can be initiated by either party, and the children should always have the freedom to call either one of their parents.

Negotiating the Settlement

Once you understand the different settlement variations that are available, you and your attorney have to figure out how to get the one that's best for you and your children. First, you need to determine what's reasonable and possible for you as a parent. There's no reason for you to push for sole custody, for example, if you really don't have the time or inclination to take on that sort of primary role with your children. So you must carefully examine your wants and capabilities and decide what you can and cannot do. After you have done that, we recommend that you sit down with your former spouse and try to work out the basics of an agreement after consulting with your lawyer. The hope is that parents can save themselves some money and at the same time begin building a working relationship with each other that will serve them well in the years to come. You and your spouse should attempt these negotiations early on in the divorce or custody process, before the case has become fraught with animosity and distrust. You should discuss visitation and custody as well as the various rights and responsibilities and see if you can find some common ground. You should be flexible within reason and be willing to listen. And for the time being, you should also forget about bringing in other issues such as money or property except as they directly relate to the kids; they will only muddy the picture and could have a negative effect on talks. If the two of you can work out a general agreement between yourselves, go back to your lawyers and try to put something on paper, which you can then study and fine tune with your respective attorneys. You must involve your lawyers at this point to make sure all relevant issues are dealt with and that there are no gaping loopholes that could cause problems later on. No one should ever sign anything without having an attorney look it over carefully.

If you and your spouse can't even agree on a basic agreement structure, bring your lawyers in and attempt to work as a group to resolve the issue. You must keep several things in mind as you are trying to cut a deal. First, you need to make sure that all issues are clearly spelled out, especially if you have some doubts about how you and your ex-wife are going to be able to deal with each other in the future. This is critical as it relates to visitation. Time and time again, people sign documents providing for "reasonable" visitation, only to discover later on that they and their former spouses had very different opinions of what constitutes "reasonable." Once the document is drawn up, you need to go over it very carefully—on your own and with your lawyer. Never hesitate to ask questions or try to make changes if you think they are important. You should not assume that the agreement your attorney has handed you is in perfect shape and ready to sign. You're the one—not your lawyer—who has to live with what's spelled out inside the document; so it behooves you to be extremely cautious and clear about what it says. Finally, you need to realize that all custody and visitation agreements are modifiable, which means they can be legally amended at the request of either parent and upon court order. That means your former wife can change her mind in a year and haul everybody back to court. However, she would have to make a compelling case showing that the change would be in the best interests of the children in order for that move to succeed.

It is also important to be reasonable in your negotiations. To start with, the woman with whom you are trying to settle is the mother of your children, and unless there is something terribly wrong with her, she deserves to play a significant role in the upbringing of your kids. And certainly the children deserve to have both their parents as involved as possible. Therefore, it is selfish to try and cut the mother out as a parent. You must remember that a custody settlement is something you and your former spouse will be living with for many years to come. It is one of the first things you try to do together as divorced or soon-to-be-divorced parents, and you can set a healthy tone of cooperation for the future by putting aside your emotional pain and frustration to figure out ways of dealing with each other. If you want to be the best possible parents down the road, you are going to have to learn how to work with each other, and what better place to start than with a settlement?

In some instances, a person involved in a divorce or custody negotiation will try to overreach. He may have the upper hand for one reason or another and try to use it to the maximum. He backs his former spouse into a corner, demanding more and more until he gets almost everything he wants. He plays on her emotional weaknesses and guilt. Perhaps she has an inferior attorney, and he takes advantage of that. Even though a joint custody arrangement might be best for all involved and would assure him of having primary physical custody of his children, he pushes for sole custody. The man may think he's winning big, but he could be setting himself up for a major fall. A parent who has been shackled with an unfair agreement is less likely to comply with all its provisions than one who is party to a more reasonable deal. The emotional angst and distress of the divorce or custody battle will likely be prolonged if he bullies his way to a favorable pact, and continued litigation is almost guaranteed. There's also the risk that people who have been unjustly stripped of a significant parenting role will disappear from their children's lives, or go completely in the opposite direction and try to abduct them. Even if a mother who has been hammered by an unfair deal remains actively involved, her psyche may be so battered by the results of her settlement that her abilities as a parent are severely compromised. You would be far wiser not to throw the knock-out punch in talks involving the children and leave something on the table for your former spouse, even if you are in a position to clobber her. It's essential to recognize that a custody battle is not about winning or losing; it's about doing what's right for the kids. They gain nothing if one of their parents is destroyed.

Remember, too, that once a settlement is reached, the process of understanding and cooperation should not suddenly stop. The agreement still has to be implemented, and both parents need to work hard to make sure they adhere to all its stipulations. It would also be constructive if the parties made a point of always dealing with each other respectfully. You should treat your ex-wife as you would like her to treat you. Let her know if there is going to be a change of plans, such as an early or late pick-up. Have the children ready to go when she comes to pick them up. Make sure they are neat, clean, and dressed properly. Try not to keep them up late the night before so they are tired and unruly for your former spouse the next day. Don't send messages through the children, and if at all possible, try to spend a little time with their mother when she comes over to get them instead of just shooing them out the door without so much as a hello. A civil postmarital relationship can be immensely helpful for both parents and kids, who certainly benefit from seeing Mom and Dad deal with each other in a friendly, positive way.

We know of one couple who managed to establish a particularly solid relationship as friends after their divorce was finalized. Not only did it make things easier for them as parents of a young girl, but it also gave their child an enormous sense of pleasure and security knowing that her mother and father not only got along but could sometimes get together and do things with her. There wasn't any hope or prospect of the parents getting back together, but that didn't seem to matter to their daughter. "Even though you guys are divorced, I still have a family," she said after spending a weekend with them during a vacation exchange.

Unfortunately, not every set of divorced parents can get along so well, and the road for some is quite rocky. One possible way of smoothing that out is therapy, either individually or as a couple. Judge Steinberg believed so strongly in the benefits of counseling for parents who have divorced or are going through the process that he insisted on it for those who settle cases in his courtroom. "I asked that they agree to monthly therapy sessions for one year," he said. "Not so they can try and get back together, but rather so they can function as parents. If I just churned out decisions and left people as they were, they'd be back in court six months later haggling over something else. What I hoped therapy would do was help them achieve an emotionally balanced divorce and take the craziness out of their behavior and what they're going through, for their benefit but mostly for the benefit of their kids. I wanted to see them get through the process with some self-respect and let go of all the anger and frustration they felt so they would work together as parents and get on with their lives. And if problems arose, they would call their therapists instead of their lawyers and resolve things in the counselor's office rather than the courtroom."

5

If You Are Unable to Settle

UNFORTUNATELY, SETTLEMENT ISN'T ALWAYS POSSIBLE, AND there comes a time when a trial is the only option left. As we have previously explained, there is nothing pretty about that experience. A custody trial is almost always an exhausting, expensive, and emotionally wrenching procedure that tests the sanity, composure, and patience of even the most well-adjusted individual. But you can't afford to get squeamish about what lies ahead. If your case is indeed going to trial and you truly believe that your children's best interests will be met by your forging ahead with your fight, you need to do everything you can to make sure you win.

It's not unusual for it to take a year from the initial legal filings for a custody trial to finally begin. Once the first witness is called, the case will likely last anywhere from five to eight days. But don't bet on those being continuous or consecutive. Unless your case is being heard before a specialty court that deals only with custody battles and will devote entire days to one dispute, it will be interrupted or delayed many times for any number of reasons. Say you are asked to appear in court at 10:00 in the morning for the start of your trial. Chances are the judge will have several other issues to contend with beforehand and won't even get to your case until noon. Then everybody will break for lunch at 1:00 and return at 2:00. Court will go back in session until 3:30, at which point there will be a fifteen-minute recess. Things will begin again at 3:45 and run until 5:00. Taken together, that doesn't leave much time for the actual trial. In addition, parents should count on at least three interruptions during the day involving other cases; it might be a woman looking for an immediate order of protection from her husband who has beaten her up the night before or a man trying to get a temporary restraining order to keep his wife from leaving town that afternoon with his children. Whatever the reason, they will occur, and as they do, they will draw your trial out even further. If your case gets the judge's undivided attention for four hours in a given day, that's a lot. One of the keys here is to be as prepared for the inevitable delays as you are for your case. Patience is an important virtue when dealing with the legal system, and you would be wise not to let the shortcomings of the process distract you from the greater task at hand, which, of course, is winning.

Trials can unfold in a variety of ways, and it's hard to predict exactly how each one will go. But we can give a rough sense of what they usually involve for both plaintiffs (the ones who filed the original actions) and defendants. For the purpose of this example, we will assume you are the plaintiff.

You will be the first one called to the stand. Your attorney asks the initial questions, and that examination, which is also known as the direct, generally lasts three to four hours. It is perhaps the most critical part of your case and your best chance to shine before the court. Next comes the cross-examination from the opposing attorney, which will certainly be hostile. Lawyers each have their own style, and different ones will approach this part of the trial in different ways. Some may be aggressive, others calm. They may jump back and forth between issues regarding the children, money, and property in an attempt to confuse a witness. They may try to provoke you so you lose your cool. Whatever tack they take, their aim is the same: to make their client look like the significantly better parent and person. All told, the cross-examination will probably last two or three hours. The plaintiff has a right of rebuttal at your point. Your lawyer will take perhaps twenty minutes to deal with any potentially harmful issues that came up. Then the defense attorney has the opportunity to rebut the rebuttal (known as a surrebuttal), which usually lasts about ten minutes.

Next, your lawyer will call two or three credibility witnesses, people who can speak on your behalf and your worthiness as a parent. These might include close friends and one or both of your parents if they live nearby and have had the opportunity to observe you with your children. Another possibility is having one of the children's former school teachers testify. (Most attorneys and therapists believe that involving a current educator in the trial might adversely affect their relationship with the children and should be avoided.) A day-care provider or religious instructor might also make sense. Each of those will spend twenty minutes to half an hour testifying. The lawyer will also call the person from the Family Relations Division who has conducted the case study if she has come down in favor of the plaintiff. He would want the court to hear how and why that decision was reached, and that testimony could take as long as two hours. If an independent therapist has worked on the case as well and filed a favorable report, it would be smart to call him to the stand.

Some attorneys like to surprise defendants by suddenly asking them to testify during that time. "I do that in about seventy percent of my cases," says one veteran matrimonial lawyer, "and my hope is to catch them off guard. I won't spend a lot of time with them, perhaps an hour. But I will go over ten good bullet points. The idea is to get them to respond to my questions before they were expecting them and before they had a chance to tell their entire story in an unfettered way." How that lawyer approaches the defendant depends on the kind of person she is. "Most times, I'll spend eighty percent of my examination describing my clients strengths and the rest of the time pointing out her weaknesses," he explains. "But if the woman clearly is bad news, and the court knows it, I might spend half my time attacking her." Just as when the plaintiff testified, the defense has the right to cross-examine all witnesses, and the same opportunities for rebuttal and surrebuttal exist. Your lawyer will probably spend no more than two full days presenting your case, at which point he will rest and turn things over to the defense.

The routine for the defendant is more or less the same; she will have a chance to present her story in testimony, and after being cross-examined, she may roll out her own witnesses. The big difference is that a defendant won't be starting her presentation until the third or fourth day of the trial, and by that point, many judges have become less patient with the proceedings. They might be stricter with their rulings or be more rushed, all of which could have an effect on how they view a case and what defendants need to do to make themselves heard. A sharp defense lawyer will look closely at how a judge is reacting to the case and adjust his strategy accordingly.

When the defendant is done, both attorneys will give their closing arguments before the judge, each of which generally lasts twenty minutes. Those final summations get big play on prime-time television shows, and clients like to hear them made. But the fact is, they mean little to the men and women on the bench. Most of the time, they have already made up their minds and are not swayed one way or another by those last words.

Rather, they are swayed by the evidence they have heard and the way the plaintiff and defendant act in their courtroom. "I tell my clients that their demeanor during the trial may be even more important than what they say," argues one attorney, and we tend to agree. To begin with, a man must dress appropriately. Coat and tie are essential, and the outfit should project a conservative, almost somber tone. "A man should look as if he is going to church," says one family court judge. Also, stay away from flashy cufflinks or expensive suits, ties, and shoes; there's no need to show a judge how wealthy you are when that same person may be making rulings on the amount of money and property you will have to give your former spouse. It's just asking for trouble. Look good, but don't look like a million. In addition, make sure you are comfortable. We know of a man who came to court on an early spring day wearing a three-piece wool suit. By noon the temperature outside had risen into the low 70s. It was even hotter in the courtroom, and with the air conditioning not yet in service, he began to perspire during his testimony. Not only did his discomfort make it hard for him to concentrate on the task at hand, but it also caused him to look unnecessarily nervous. That might well have made the judge wonder: Is this guy sweating because he is not telling the truth? Confidence, but not cockiness, can also help a lot, and the court should get the sense that you have faith in yourself and your abilities as a father.

Some other pointers worth keeping in mind:

- Don't chew gum in the courtroom. It seems to irritate every judge we have met.

- Don't whisper while the judge is talking. And never utter remarks under your breath after the judge has spoken or make faces at what the judge, a lawyer, or a witness has said.

- Stand up when the judge walks into the courtroom, and don't sit down before he does.

- Make appropriate eye contact with the judge throughout the proceeding.

- Never lose your temper in front of the judge, no matter what happens. You are trying to prove your worth as a parent, and no one is going to side with a parent who comes unglued in the courtroom or in the halls during a break. We have seen witnesses scream at their lawyers during testimony, hurl insults and threats at their former spouses, and knock the court recorder's microphone to the ground in frustration. Their cases all suffered as a result. Those outbursts made the men appear violent and out of control, which are not the traits a good parent would normally project. The key is to remain calm and collected in the face of terrific stress. Judges know how difficult custody battles are, and they will appreciate the plaintiff or defendant who handles it all in a measured and rational way.

- You should also be aware that a judge may be watching you even before you ever step up to the stand. It's common for plaintiffs, defendants, and their attorneys to wait around in the courtroom for their turn while other cases are being heard. If that happens, be very careful with your behavior. Don't noisily read a newspaper or magazine. Don't slip on a Walkman and start listening to music. And don't laugh or joke with a friend sitting nearby. Don't do anything that might aggravate the person who will be hearing your case.

- Judges are very particular about what goes on in their courtrooms, and they are not afraid to enforce their own sets of rules. Do what they tell you, and do it pleasantly. We once saw a man who was about to begin a custody battle for his son stand up before a judge and address him with his hands in his pants pocket. It was his first day in court, he was understandably nervous, and he didn't know any better. But that didn't matter to the judge, who looked at him sharply and barked, "Take your hands out of your pockets." Not only was he enforcing a standard rule in his courtroom, but he was doing it in an arrogant way, as if he was trying to show everybody who was boss. The man didn't like what the judge had done and had every reason to take offense at his tone. But instead he nodded politely and did as he was told. He understood that the judge was indeed king in that courtroom and getting angry at him or showing it in the slightest way wasn't going to help his fight for his son. So he swallowed his pride and backed right down.

- Try not to get disappointed by the process. The delays can be maddening at times, the rules of evidence confusing, the tactics of the opposing attorney unfair. You have to shake off the negatives and maintain your energy, confidence, and focus. It's your best chance at surviving it all—and for winning.

Some attorneys also urge their clients to watch how a judge conducts himself in court during another trial. How does he act with the plaintiff and defendant? with the lawyers? Does he ask a lot of questions? How does he rule on objections? Does he appear pro-father or pro-mother? Sometimes, it's helpful just to see the judge in his element and observe how he handles himself, so you will know what to expect and feel more comfortable. Again, anything to improve demeanor.

Once your trial starts and you begin testifying, you must remember to keep your answers under cross-examination short and to the point and never volunteer information. In addition, you should always look to your lawyer before answering any question from the opposition to make sure he is not about to object. You certainly don't want to respond to a query the judge is about to disallow. It's also not a bad idea to pay close attention to the questions the opposing attorney is asking your spouse or any of the other witnesses, whether under direct or cross-examination. You may pick up some things that your attorney can exploit later on in the trial. If that happens, you should let your lawyer know right away by writing him a note and passing it over. A smart attorney will appreciate the feedback and use whatever he can to better his case. Good information can be an enormous help.

There are several other ways you can help your cause. Before each court appearance, you should review all pleadings and depositions to make sure there will be no inconsistencies in your story when you take the stand. You might also discover that your wife has left things out of her financial affidavit, for example, or that she is not telling the truth about something that happened while you were together. The idea is to be as prepared as possible so that your attorney may argue your case and attack hers. In addition, you and your lawyer must be ready to tell your entire story in court. You should never assume a judge has read one sentence in the file about the case prior to sitting down on the bench that first day. Rather, they must approach it as if the court hasn't heard a thing about the dispute before. That way, nothing is inadvertently left out.

JUDGES

Judges are difficult to read sometimes, and you can never be exactly sure what they are thinking. We thought we could shed some light on their attitudes, however, by relating what three very different members of the bench told us they look for in a custody case and what they say helps them to make their decisions. The first person we spoke with is a woman in her early forties who talked primarily about the children involved. "I don't think it's a good idea for a judge to see the kids beforehand," she says. "But I do like it when parents or their attorneys give me a picture of their children. I put it on the bench when I am hearing a case so I can remember what the proceedings are all about. The children become more real to me, and I can visualize them better."

We then asked her what decides a case in a person's favor. "When I am looking at parents, I am looking for the one who exhibits the greater degree of maturity and selflessness," she says. "The one who is making all kinds of time for the kids. Different things happen to people when marriages break up. Some get so consumed by anger and grief that they seem to lose touch with their kids, while others stay right with their children and routines as parents. They start seeing a therapist when the marriage is falling apart and try to take care of whatever problems they have. They show a desire and ability to get beyond the hurt of the divorce, to not be so consumed by their own troubles, and to do what's best for the kids. You see that in little ways, such as not sending messages back and forth through the children, not arguing in front of them, and not bad mouthing the other parent. Some parents step up to the plate and some

don't. Some are emotionally mature and some aren't. I'm looking for the parent who is more emotionally mature. And that
has nothing to do with gender."

Our second judge is a man in his mid-sixties. "I like to ask the
parents why they want custody of their children," he says.
"Invariably a number of them start telling me what the child
means to them, but that's not the answer I want to hear. I don't
care so much about the parents' needs; I'm concerned about
their children and what's best for them. I'm looking out for their
best interests.

"I am always impressed when a lawyer throws a softball
across to his own client instead of hurling a high hard one into
the face of the other side," the judge continues. "I like to see
someone avoid doing damage to the other side. There's that
blood lust that some people have in court, and they will run
with it. They will tell you horrible things about the other person,
and sometimes I'm embarrassed by what people will say and do
in court. They will take loving things they learned in marriage
and beat each other over the head with them in a custody case.

"I have trouble seeing the client beyond the lawyer on occasion," he adds. "Some parents make the mistake of hiring a
street fighter, thinking that a hard-nosed gunslinger will help
them. But they don't recognize the terrible burden they are
putting on a judge by making you look beyond that behavior in
order to see what the client really is like. If there are a lot of
sneering questions, a lot of mean-spiritedness on the part of the
attorney, it is very hard to differentiate between [the attorney
and the client]. And that makes it difficult to decide where the
child should go. A parent's best bet is probably hiring a lawyer

that most accurately reflects the nature of their own personality and behavior."

The third member of our judicial trio is another man who is in his early seventies and nearing retirement. "One thing that is very important to me is dress," he says. "I'm impressed by people who care enough to come to court dressed appropriately. That's a prevailing view, I believe. It may sound old-fashioned, but earrings and long hair for men are an issue for me as well. I just don't like them."

"Once the plaintiff or defendant is on the stand, he or she should position themselves in a way that they can look at their lawyer and turn to me on occasion," the judge adds. "I like eye contact. If there are potential witnesses familiar with the case in the courtroom, they should not make any gestures or comments while the trial is going on. I will usually say something about it, and it's the sort of thing that can be held against the witness. Frankly, I think it's better for character witnesses to be outside the courtroom and come in only when it's time for them to take the stand. Character witnesses have some bearing as far as I'm concerned, but too many is too many. I don't think there's any need for more than two for each side.

"To me, the best evidence a father can present is his participation in the children's lives up to the point of the trial," he explains. "He doesn't have to be the coach of his kid's Little League team, but I would like to see that he's gone to as many games as possible. If he has a sincere interest in the children, then that's what's most important to me. But judges do have a predisposition in many cases that if the mother's a fit person, she should have custody of the children. I think a mother has to screw up to lose custody of the child, and that's one of the things a judge is trying to decide: what is in the best interests of the children? If a mother is working fulltime and the father is the house-husband, however, the father should have custody because he has the time to be there.

"I also don't like mudslinging," the judge says. "And I don't like people losing their temper in my courtroom. They should refer to each other by their given family name. Sure, I understand that this is all a battle sometimes, and people want to do everything they can to win their case. That's fine within reason. Just don't sling any mud."

The Decision

After all the evidence is heard in a custody case, it usually takes the judge another month or so to hand down a written decision. (Most judges pass the news along to the lawyers involved, who then get in touch with their clients. Some members of the bench, however, have the bad habit of calling both parties into the courtroom and reading their decision before them. It can be a devastating experience and should be avoided if at all possible.) Though talking to your wife may be the last thing you want to do at this point, it might still make sense to pursue the possibility of a settlement. Perhaps some things came up in the trial that softened her stance. Or maybe you see that you were being unrealistic and asking for too much. Both sides know how the outside evaluators and witnesses feel, and you should have a fairly good idea of what the judge might do. It makes sense then for you to look at your positions once again and see if you can't somehow work out a solution before the judge imposes one of his own. You still have some time left.

6

CASE STUDIES: HOW OTHERS HAVE FARED IN THE PROCESS

THE CUSTODY PROCESS RARELY WORKS THE SAME WAY twice, and that's because so much is dependent on the specifics of each case, the abilities of the lawyers who have been retained, the competence of the Family Relations unit handling the study, the personality of the judge overseeing the proceedings, and the sensibilities of the parents. It's not really possible to look at the outcome of one battle and know just how another will turn out. Still, you might find it helpful to see what has happened in other cases and how individuals in those situations fared, especially when it comes to plotting strategy and understanding how desperate and irrational former spouses can become. It can also be comforting to know that others have fought through the system before you and come out in decent shape. In addition, you will probably feel an almost perverse relief when you learn of other people who are having much greater problems with their cases; it will likely give you some hope for your own success and keep you from getting too despondent or discouraged.

With all that in mind, we have selected four case studies that describe a series of difficult situations. Two have been resolved as of this printing, while the others were still to be hashed out in the courtroom. And all of them have tested the patience—and sanity—of the men involved.

CRAIG AND SUSAN

Craig and Susan Johnson were in their late twenties when they took their four young children to South Carolina for an Easter vacation. Their seven-year marriage had been troubled and volatile at times, but it never got so bad that they discussed divorce or separation. Like many couples with young children, they seemed to muddle on as best they could and deal with the many minor problems that cropped up. One of the biggest issues of their marriage was Susan's relationship with her in-laws; she felt they controlled Craig, especially his domineering mother. That worried her as they drove to South Carolina because they would be staying at her in-laws' house. The last thing she had wanted to do was spend a week with Craig's parents and sisters. But she was almost there.

Things started to go bad almost from the moment they arrived. Craig's mother assigned a variety of tasks for Susan to complete over the week, which upset Susan. She went right to the refrigerator, from which she pulled out a bottle of white wine and started drinking. She had several glasses over the next hour and then suddenly blew up. She started screaming at her mother-in-law and then lashed out at other members of the family. Craig managed to calm her down before bed, but sometime in the middle of the night Susan got all her children up, loaded them into the family car, and took off for their home. As soon as she arrived, she called one of the area's top matrimonial lawyers and arranged to meet him the following morning, which was a Sunday. Their strategy was to go into court on Monday and get a restraining order giving her immediate custody of the children and charging Craig with physical and extreme emotional distress. She claimed, among other things, that her husband had physically abused her the night of the altercation at her in-law's.

Susan and her lawyer presented their case before a judge on Monday without Craig even being in the courtroom. Despite his absence and the fact that she could not prove there was any actual physical abuse on the Friday before, she was able to obtain the restraining order. The court served papers on Craig the next day, summoning him to a hearing that Friday. He immediately hired an attorney, who advised him to try to contact his children by telephone. The first time he tried, Susan hung up. Craig called six or seven more times and was finally told by his wife's mother that the restraining order even covered telephone conversations. Here was a man who had been a model parent, who had an excellent relationship with his children, and he wasn't even allowed to speak to them on the telephone.

At Friday's hearing Susan showed up with three friends, all of whom testified that Craig had repeatedly threatened her over the years. He vehemently denied that, but the judge didn't believe him and made the order stick, with some modifications. He decided to allow five minutes of telephone contact with the children three times a week and permitted him to see them for three hours on Saturday afternoons at a local park, but only with a third-party supervisor. Craig was devastated and couldn't believe that in less than one week he had gone from putting his children to bed every night and cooking them breakfast in the mornings to having supervised weekly visits, all because his wife had snapped out.

The court appointed an attorney for the children, and the parents put aside their differences long enough to retain an independent therapist for them as well. In addition, the court referred the case to Family Relations for an investigation that took almost six months. During that time, Craig hardly saw his children, and he learned that their mother was constantly trying to poison their relationship with him by making derogatory comments about him, including a claim that Daddy had a young girlfriend and preferred to spend his time with her and not them. Nothing could have been further from the truth, but that was the story they were getting.

After six months, the children's attorney and therapist presented their reports, as did Family Relations. And they all came down in favor of the father. Susan refused to accept the findings or enter into settlement talks. So the judge scheduled a trial three months later. Just before that was to take place, the mother claimed to have a nervous breakdown, resulting in another three-month delay. But this time, the trial took place, and things went very well for Craig. Susan came across badly and had several outbursts on the stand. The judge was horrified by her behavior and ruled that the parents should have joint custody, but the children should live most of the time with Craig.

Although that battle was over, Susan continued making life miserable for Craig, often picking up the children late, changing schedules haphazardly, and putting down their father in front of them. Craig has still not gotten over the fact that it took him a year to resume a normal life with his children, and the legal fees for both himself and Susan had soared, at last count, to almost $400,000. If that money had been invested wisely, it could have easily put all four children through college.

BILL AND PEGGY

Thirty-two-year-old Bill Paine and his wife Peggy had been married six years and had three children all under the age of seven when she threw him out of their house and told him never to come back. "We had had some problems over the years, ranging from my working too hard to us not having enough money," Bill says. "Plus, she couldn't stand my parents, and it was a major ordeal just to have dinner with them. But I didn't think things between us were so bad that we needed to split up."

Actually, the marriage had been deteriorating for some time, and Peggy was becoming more and more dissatisfied. "It got to the point where she wouldn't allow my parents to see the kids except when she needed a babysitter," Bill says. "She also had issues with my sister, and they'd get into some pretty nasty scraps. I still don't understand why things got so bad between them all, and Peggy has never been able to articulate to me or anyone else what she had against them. But whatever the reasons, she was adamant about staying as far away from my family as possible."

As their marriage entered its sixth year, Peggy had also begun arguing with Bill a lot, mostly over money and the fact that she had had to go back to work in order to help make ends meet. "She was furious about that, and would scream at me in front of the kids every morning as she got ready to go to her job, complaining that I was a no-good bum who was making her go to work while none of her sisters and few of her girlfriends had to."

The tension within Bill's family built throughout the year, and then things exploded shortly after the Christmas holidays. His parents were upset that they could only see their grandchildren on an irregular and infrequent basis and frustrated that their many requests for more time with Bill's kids were met with Peggy's cold indifference. So they hired a lawyer and filed an action for greater visitation. "It wasn't long after that that Peggy marched into the place where I worked and started screaming at me," Bill says. "She accused me of not caring about my kids and said I had chosen my family over ours. Then she told me not to come home that night."

And so began Bill and Peggy's unofficial separation. "It was a really strange time," he recalls. "Sometimes, she would call and yell at me for staying away from the house and not caring enough about her and the kids, and on other occasions she'd say she didn't want anything to do with me." They were able to get together twice a week for the next several months and spend time as a family, either over dinner or lunch. "It was very amicable for a while," he says. "Every now and again I would babysit for her, and I got to see the kids at least twice, if not three times a week. I also called the kids almost every night before they went to bed. The only real problem I had was that Peggy very rarely let me see the girls alone. We were almost always together with them."

But the niceties ended when Peggy had legal separation papers served on Bill that fall, about six months after she had thrown him out. "I was depicted as a fall-down drunk, drug addict, and a deadbeat dad because I wasn't always able to pay the rent for the house she lived in with the children on time," he says. But the worse part was that Peggy was demanding full custody of the children and did not want Bill to see them at all. "She was able to convince the judge hearing our case that I was trouble, and so all he would give me at the time was supervised visitation," Bill says. "I could see them twice a week at their house for a couple of hours each time. I was not allowed to take them off the premises, and I could not see them by myself."

It was a rough fall. Peggy didn't let Bill see his children on Thanksgiving and gave him only a couple of hours with them on Christmas Eve. "They came over to my parents' house with their mother, and you can imagine how uncomfortable that was," he explains. "But Peggy wouldn't let them come over on their own. And when they did arrive, it was very awkward. Any time that my parents or sister held the girls or had them sit in their laps, Peggy would try to take them away, saying they were supposed to be there with me. I went back to court on a couple of occasions and complained that she was not complying with the visitation schedule and asked for more time. But she told the judge each time that she hadn't held the kids back at all. Once she had the audacity to say that I could see them any time I wanted. But when I tried to take her up on that, all she did was scream and yell at me in front of the children. It was horrible, and I eventually decided to stop trying to visit them outside of the scheduled supervised visits because I thought it was so bad for them to have to see their mother act that way toward me."

It got to the point that Bill couldn't see his children at all. "We had a court date one afternoon, and right there in the courthouse she started screaming at me," he says. "I didn't say a thing, but the sheriff grabbed her and said she'd be arrested if she didn't settle down. We tried to work some stuff out in court that day, but she and her lawyer disagreed with anything we said, so we left without having resolved a thing. Ten minutes later I was walking to my car and all of a sudden Peggy drove by and tried to hit me with her car. I jumped out of the way just in time, so she threw her car into park, hopped out, and started berating me right there on the street, yelling at me, hitting me, kicking me as I walked. I kept on moving toward my car, and when I got there she took one of her keys and ran it along the outside of the door on the passenger side. And then she jumped into the front seat and started going at me there as I tried to start the car. I backed up quickly and could think of only one thing to do, and that was drive her down to her father's office, which wasn't too far away. The whole time she kept kicking and screaming at me, but I managed to get her there and get her out of the car. I was bleeding like crazy from my hand when I drove off, and the next day I had some bruises on my arms, legs, and side where she had hit and kicked me. And you know what she did? She filed a complaint against me for assault and was able to get a restraining order from a judge, without me or my lawyer even being present, stipulating that I stay away from her and the children because I had attacked her after our court date. She was saying that I was the dangerous one, and the court believed her."

Four months after that incident, Bill has still not seen his children. He is only allowed to speak with them on the telephone twice a week. "It doesn't always work out so well," he says. "One time one of my daughters got on the phone and told me to go to hell. Peggy says that the kids don't want to see me or my parents. On a couple of occasions I called at the prescribed time, which is 7:30 P.M., and no one answered. When I did finally get through around 10:00, Peggy picked up the phone, told me I was a drunk or something to that effect, and then hung up. She has Caller ID and knew it was me trying to get through. So she would just let it ring."

Bill pauses for a moment as he recounts these horror stories, and then shakes his head and sighs. "I know that I was not the best husband at times," he says. "I also know that I was not the best father. But I have never done anything to hurt my wife or my children, and I certainly don't deserve the treatment I have received for the past two years. It's ridiculous how slow the courts have worked and how easy it was for Peggy to get orders separating me from my children. She's the one who has been violent, who has tried to poison the kids' minds, who has kept them not only from their father but also their grandparents. And yet I'm the one who is viewed as the bad guy. I just don't think it's right."

As of this printing, Bill's case was yet to be resolved. But

Family Relations has recommended that his parents get regular visitation with his daughters. "It's taken a while, but at least it's a step in the right direction," he says. "Hopefully, my time will come someday soon."

ERIC AND MARTHA

Eric Bryan was twenty-six years old when he married Martha Nichols, and four years later they began having children. The first three came about fourteen months apart, and then they waited almost two years before having number four. Eric worked as a marketing executive and Martha as a real estate agent, and they lived together in a small New England town. To most of their friends, they seemed a happy couple who enjoyed a good life together. But by the time their youngest, a boy, had come onto the scene, they were having serious problems.

"Truth be told, the troubles had started long before our son was born," Eric says. "In fact, we had had difficulties with our marriage almost from the beginning. The main issue as I saw it was that Martha was a very abusive, manipulative and controlling person. She expected me home at night from work at 6 P.M., and if I was five minutes late, all hell would break loose. Same if I was on a business trip and didn't check in on a regular basis. She would call endlessly, just to see where I was and what I was doing. It got worse and worse over the years, and at some point I just got inured to the whole thing. It was like being shell-shocked, and I learned how to put up with it."

But Eric's ability to deal with Martha's incessant badgering began to waver once they began having kids. "Things just became more and more difficult to bear," he says. "She had a very volatile personality and had no restraint in how she spent our money. She stopped working once we started a family, and our debts just mushroomed." At the same time, Martha's outbursts began taking a violent turn. "I remember one time she threw a pair of cocktail glasses at my feet when I had come home half an hour late from work, right in front of the children," Eric says. "The glasses shattered on the floor, and all three of our kids started crying."

It was a few days after that glass-throwing incident that Eric went to talk to an attorney about the possibility of divorce. He also began seeing a marriage counselor, though without Martha, who refused to go with him. "Things had become unbearable, and I was getting ready to pack things in," Eric says. "And then Martha told me she was pregnant with our son. We talked about having an abortion, which in some ways would have made sense, seeing how bad our situation had become. But she was adamantly opposed."

Martha had their fourth child in the winter of 1992, and a few months after his birth, she and Eric had their first physical confrontation. "She had one of her typical explosions over some stupid thing," Eric says. "She was yelling and screaming at me, telling me to hit her, taunting me. She threw a lamp at me, which shattered on the floor, and then she threw a drink. I backed her into one of our guest bedrooms and just slapped her across the face twice, telling her to stop all the nonsense. Things broke up after that, and we went to sleep in separate rooms. And the next day when I got back from work, the cops were there. She had called them to get me, but after they heard both our stories and listened to our nanny, who had witnessed the whole thing, they arrested both of us. Fortunately, all charges were dropped, and we were back in the house together."

It was another year before things heated up again. "Martha was ticked off because I had to go on a business trip and wouldn't let me leave the house," Eric says. "I mean, I could have left if I had pushed her out of the way in front of our children, but I didn't want to do that. So I called the cops, and they came and allowed me to get out of the house. I went on that trip, and when I got back I filed for divorce."

Right after Eric made that move, he took his four children and moved into his parents' house and left Martha in the marital home. "I did that for a couple of reasons," he says. "One, I was convinced that Martha was mentally unstable and something of a threat to our children. And two, I had always played a major role in the kids' upbringing, even more than her, and thought they would be better off with me for that reason as well. I was always the one who got the kids up in the morning. Martha never nursed, and I did most of the midnight feedings as well. I remember one evening when I was so tired I asked Martha to feed our youngest. She went ahead and did it but couldn't get him to go back to sleep. So I got up, held him in my arms, and he dozed right off."

Martha didn't sit idly by when Eric left with the children, and she immediately hired an attorney. "That night they were able to get a judge to sign a restraining order against me saying I was a danger to her and the children," Eric says. "She cited three or four incidents on the complaint, only one of which was even remotely true. And the next day, a Monday, the police came to my parents' house and took my children away. I wasn't allowed to see them for two weeks and had to go to court at the end of that time to argue my case."

Eric had asked for sole custody when he initially file for divorce, but once he had lost them altogether, he began to modify his stance. "I was a little more willing to negotiate, to be flexible, when I went into court that day, because I hadn't seen my children in a while and I was worried about how much time I would get with them at all," he says. By the end of the day he had agreed to a joint custody arrangement and a temporary visitation schedule giving him the children every other weekend and every Wednesday night for dinner. "Everybody referred to it as a temporary arrangement which would be altered as soon as we could work out some more of the details," Eric says. "And I thought it was fine because I just wanted to see my children again." Only later did Eric understand that temporary custody arrangements are anything but temporary. "We signed that deal in April, and it was almost two years before that 'temporary' setup was changed," he says. "Almost two years before I could see my children more than a few times a month." Around that same time, Eric and Martha had a hearing about their finances, and a judge ordered him to pay, again on a "temporary basis," $2,500 a month in child support and $1,000 a month in alimony. "My net monthly income at the time was $4,000," he says, "so that left me a grand total of $500 a month spending money. How did anybody expect me to live on that?"

Eventually, a judge asked Family Relations to conduct a study of the case and appointed an attorney for the minor children. The study took about four months, and much to Eric's delight, the social workers at Family Relations came down in his favor. "But what was really interesting was that even though they had ruled in my favor, the woman who was representing my children kept urging me to settle and not go to trial," he says. "She wanted me to give Martha the house and more money, all because I was a man, and she said I wouldn't have a very good chance in court as a result of that. But I told her to forget it. I was fighting all the way because I believed so strongly that it was the best thing for the children. And I really believed I had a strong case."

Eric faced two separate trials. One dealt with the custody issue while the other involved finances. "We were able to settle the custody arrangement after the Family Relations people reported their findings on the study," Eric says. "My wife got the kids every other weekend and one weekday night for dinner as well as five weeks in the summer. And she had ninety days to leave the house. I was so happy that we had worked that out and couldn't believe that nearly two years after filing for divorce and spending more than $100,000 in legal fees that I had gotten what I wanted all along."

But then there were the financial issues, and those would be just as difficult to resolve. Martha, it had been determined, was manic depressive, and she claimed in the trial that she was too sick to work and needed $1,000 a month in alimony. In addition, she would not be able to pay any child support. "I couldn't believe it when her attorney brought in a therapist and said that she was too sick to work, when Martha had spent most of the past two years arguing that she should be the custodial parent," Eric says. Eventually, they settled on $400 a month in alimony and a one-year grace period in which the mother would pay no child support. After that she would have to help out. "The new custody arrangement began on January 1, 1995, but Martha didn't move out of the marital house for another three months," Eric says. "And when she did, she took all the furniture, even though we were supposed to have divided everything fifty-fifty. But at that point I really didn't care. Having my children was the most important thing."

Having those kids, however, cost Eric dearly. "I spent more than sixty days in court over this," he says. "I watched my children get taken away from me in a police car. I saw myself get ruined financially and, at the moment, I am technically bankrupt. My house is in foreclosure and there are three mortgages on my home. The kids are all here, doing well in school and seemingly fine. But I wonder how all of this has affected them, and I feel terrible that they had to go through all this."

As he looks back on his ordeal, Eric feels both angry and frustrated. "Some things happened in court that I could not believe," he says. "To take those kids away from me the way the judge did, without even hearing my side of things or giving me a chance to argue my case, was ridiculous. And it was almost criminal the way that 'temporary' custody arrangement lasted for nearly two years, and how they were able to take almost ninety percent of my net income away during that time frame as well. I doubt they would have done any of that to a woman. I also couldn't believe how the court never seemed to care that much about the kids. Rarely did I hear anybody talk about doing what was in the children's best interests. Most of the time, they seemed to be concerned with Martha's rights, the mother's rights, while the kids' were secondary."

Eric stops talking for a minute and shakes his head in disbelief as he thinks back to the battle he fought for so long. "A man would be in jail for the stuff Martha has done," he says. "She's lied consistently in court. She has committed assaults. She has not paid the child support money she owes me. And she rarely sees the kids. She has been able to act in the most outrageous way throughout this entire process, and was always given the benefit of the doubt. Would that have been the same way for a man?"

Eric waits awhile before he answers. "I don't think so," he says. "I really don't think so."

Scott and Missy

Thirty-eight-year-old Scott Barnes separated from his wife Missy in the summer of 1994, after twelve years of marriage and four children. "Things started falling apart for us because of a lack of communication and understanding that only worsened over time," he says. "And then Missy decided after a couple of years of therapy that she didn't want me in her life anymore. She wanted me out, and she did all she could to make that happen."

Scott remembers coming home from work one night and getting into an argument with Missy after they had put the children to bed. "We went at it pretty good, yelling and whatnot," he says. "Then all of a sudden she calls the police. The cops arrive, and she says that I've hit her and am being threatening toward her. I say nothing has happened, but they believe what she says and haul me off to jail. I hadn't touched her, but I was on my way to the slammer. I spent the night there, in a small-town jail, and the next morning she came down to bail me out."

The two of them drove back to the house and sat in the driveway talking for a while. "She was reasonably apologetic about what had happened the night before, and then I said I wanted to take our youngest boy out for breakfast," Scott recalls. "For some reason that started to set her off again, and she began threatening me, saying she would call the cops if I didn't have our son back home by a certain time. At that point I really didn't care what time she wanted us back, and my son and I headed down to a nearby coffee shop for a bite to eat. We ate some bacon and eggs and were having a great time, when a friend walked into the coffee shop and told me the police were looking for me. It seems that Missy had called the cops and told them I had kidnapped our son."

Scott brought his son back home and then went down to the police station to explain what was going on. Later that day, he met his wife at a friend's house. "I was hoping we could reach some sort of an understanding, but she wanted nothing to do with me," Scott explains. "She told me she was going to call the cops again if I tried to stay in the house. So I went home, packed up a bag of clothes, and began staying at that same friend's house. That's how our separation began."

Scott assumed Missy would be fair about visitation while he was gone until the two of them could work out a formal arrangement. "But she wouldn't let me anywhere near the kids," he says. "And she wouldn't even let me talk to them on the phone." Scott didn't see his children for more than three months. "It took us that long to get a court date," he says. "I tried to force her to let me see them before then, but nothing worked."

Missy didn't hold back when she finally presented her case in court. "She asked for ninety percent of my net monthly income for child support and alimony, as well as sole custody of the children," Scott explains. "She also asked that I not be permitted to see the kids, claiming that I was violent and unpredictable. What evidence did she have of that? The calls to the police, the claims that I had hit her, the claim that I had tried to kidnap our son—she had set me up, and all that worked against me."

The two sides began negotiating and eventually worked out an agreement. But in retrospect, Scott thinks he made a bad move. "I gave up sole custody of the children," he says. "I did that for a couple of reasons. For one thing, I really never believed that Missy would do anything to hold the kids back from me, even after all the stuff that had gone on around the time that we separated. That was naive of me, I know, but at the time, I just couldn't imagine her doing something like that. And secondly, I just didn't think I would get joint custody, let alone full, if I had tried to fight for that. Missy was being completely unreasonable, and I figured it was better to give in than keep fighting because it would all be for naught." In the end, Scott signed a twenty-two-page agreement that gave Missy sole custody and him visitation every other weekend as well as three uninterrupted weeks in the summer. "It wasn't perfect by any means," he remembers. "But it gave me access to the children again, and it was a hell of a lot better than not seeing them at all."

Unfortunately for him, problems cropped up right away. "The ink from our signatures hadn't dried, and she was already causing problems," Scott says. "First she tried to have our visitation time reduced, claiming I continually threatened her. On several occasions she didn't bring the children over to my house as scheduled, leaving me high and dry. Other times she'd show up late dropping them off and come back early to get them. I tried everything, from court orders to injunctions, to try to get some compliance. But everything with the legal system seemed to take so long, and nothing really worked."

Scott got so frustrated one time that he faxed a letter to his former wife demanding that she abide by the visitation and threatening to bring the sheriff over with him the next time he came to get his children so there wouldn't be any trouble. "In retrospect, it was a dumb thing to do," he says. "But I was so tired and angry at all the obstacles Missy kept putting up."

The fax enabled her to put up one more obstacle. She sent a copy to the lawyer the court had appointed for the children, saying it proved her contention that Scott was both crazy and violent, and a judge suspended visitation for six weeks while he tried to sort out the situation. Eventually, Scott won back his rights to visitation, but that didn't stop Missy from giving him a hard time about the kids and trying to hurt their relationship with him. "She kept saying that the children didn't want to see me," Scott says. "That was a recurring theme of hers, and that's why she wouldn't let them come over to my house. I'd leave my home after a nice weekend with them, and everybody would be laughing and talking on the way back to Missy's. And then two days later, my ex-wife tells me that the children don't want to get on the phone. How can it always be that way?"

Sadly, Scott is still fighting Missy for proper access to his children. "It makes me sick what has happened," he says. "She keeps going back to court and coming up with reasons for me not to see the children. One time, it was that I was beating them and locking them in darkened closets as punishment. I got remarried, and Missy claimed that my new wife was hitting the children. If Missy and I got into an argument when we were exchanging the kids, she would call to our oldest, who is now ten, and tell her to come listen how Daddy was being mean to Mommy. And she has never kept me informed about what is going on with our kids during the times I don't have them. I can't even tell you what nursery school my youngest son is in because she hasn't told me.

"I feel totally helpless about all of this," Scott explains. "She can say whatever she wants, and people in the courthouse believe her, at least for a while. It's all 'He said, she said,' and the courts have very little interest, it seems, in doing anything in favor of the father if he's accused of being violent or threatening in any way. But who has done more to harm these children? I was never the model husband or father, but I loved my children and I wanted to do the best for them. It's their mother who is perpetuating all the legal problems, who is keeping the children from their father, who is doing everything she can to damage that relationship. Their mother—the same person the courts keep saying is the more competent parent. It doesn't make a lot of sense, does it?"

When asked what advice he has for men facing similar problems, Scott quickly responds. "A man should never give up his rights to some form of custody," he says. "Go for full or joint, but he should never give up sole to his wife. Unless, of course, he wants nothing to do with his children. I assumed my wife would be reasonable; I assumed Missy would encourage our children's relationship with me; and I assumed she would keep me informed of what was going on in their lives and consult me as decisions needed to be made on things like doctors and schools. But none of that has happened, and I have regretted the way I trusted her to be fair ever since."

Most men who have been through custody battles seem to have a sense of regret when the ordeal is over. Regret that they weren't properly prepared. Regret that they didn't fight hard enough. Regret that they didn't understand their rights and blindly trusted their ex-wives to do the right thing. What each of these case studies demonstrates is that there is no shortage of trouble that can crop up along the way, whether the result of a disgruntled former spouse or a flawed legal system. The best thing you can do is learn from what has happened to men like these and try to make sure you don't have to go through the same thing yourself.

7

SADLY, CUSTODY BATTLES DON'T ALWAYS END WHEN the judge has made his ruling or the parents have struck an agreement on their own. Fathers and mothers move to different states, change jobs, get remarried. Any one of these developments can upset an arrangement that is already in place and create an entirely new set of problems and dynamics. There are also parents who remain angry about what happened during the legal battle and do everything they can to subvert the ruling or settlement. Alimony or child support checks are constantly late, and visitation schedules arbitrarily altered or ignored. Appeals can be filed and modifications of agreements may be sought if either parent isn't pleased with the way the case turned out or if they feel that changes such as a new spouse or job warrant changes in the custody arrangements. The big question for men is how to contend with these issues and concerns. What are their rights, for example, if their former wives try to move out of state with their children? if they have new boyfriends or husbands they do not approve of? if they keep holding back the kids for visitation? if they try to appeal a ruling that has not gone in their favor? And what if a father wants to appeal or move out of state if he has primary custody of the children? Any number of issues can arise after a ruling or settlement, and the man who knows his rights and how to exercise them will be able to weather the turbulence they often cause better than most.

APPEALS

One of the first things a parent thinks about when the former spouse has prevailed in a custody trial is appeal. (Negotiated settlements may not be appealed, though they can be set aside if, for example, one of the parties has defrauded the other.) He believes the judge has wronged him. He feels the Family Relations worker has made a poor report. He is sure the children's attorney had a bias in favor of the other parent. And he is convinced that his former spouse pulled the wool over everyone's eyes. "I need to get another judge to hear this case," he thinks. "I'm going to take this all the way to the United States Supreme Court if I have to," he argues. He makes big plans to mount a counteroffensive and fight the battle all over again. This time, he is going to do it differently. This time, he is going to win.

Unfortunately, the chances of his pulling that off are slim. National surveys show that appealing a custody decision is successful at most 10 percent of the time, mainly because appellate courts are loathe to reverse trial court findings in which the presiding judge has had the opportunity to listen to all the witnesses, take in all the other evidence, and watch how the father and mother handled themselves throughout the process. In the rare instance that an appellate court does grant an appeal, the decision of the original judge will not be overturned; rather, the case will go back to trial before a new judge, and the process will start all over. If that happens, litigants need to know they will not be able to present additional testimony before the appellate court; the judge will make his ruling after reviewing the trial transcripts and briefs provided by the attorneys but will call no one else on the stand.

In addition to being fruitless in most cases, an appeal can be extremely expensive and time consuming. The person filing could easily spend as much as $30,000 for his attorney alone, and there's the good chance that he would also have to cover the legal expenses of the former spouse he has dragged back into court. As for the time factor, an appeal generally takes a year, though it can last longer.

Another negative is that an appeal can backfire on litigants looking for a better deal because it may open up the entire case. If, for example, a man has successfully argued that Judge #1 did not give him enough custody or visitation, there's nothing to keep Judge #2 on a remand from ruling that he also didn't give his former spouse enough alimony or child support money. Anyone who exposes himself that way could come out in a lot worse shape. So it's important that a man look carefully at what he got in the initial ruling and determine whether he can really afford to open up the process again before forging ahead with another fight. Many times, he is better off simply living with what he has.

In fact, living with a custody arrangement is often the most productive step parents can take after a trial. The legal process has taken a lot of time and effort. It has cost an enormous amount of money. And it has created all sorts of stress and tension for those involved–mother, father, and children alike. Before filing an appeal, you must look carefully not only at yourself but also at the other people a new custody battle will impact and decide how badly another year of fighting will hurt them all and whether it's in anybody's best interest to head back to court. It's especially important to ask whether the children will really benefit from the added trauma of new litigation. Instead of fighting another destructive battle, you and your ex-wife would be better off devoting all that time and energy to working with the ruling that has been made and getting on with your lives. It is still possible for the noncustodial parent to maintain a good relationship with his or her children, provided both parents cooperate. It may not always be easy and it may require some work. But it can be done. And it is certainly recommended.

Are there any times when an appeal does make sense? Of course. You can use the prospect of an appeal as a tool to negotiate a more favorable visitation arrangement, for example, or to get some relief on alimony or child support payments. But that tactic only works if the ex-wife feels she might have some exposure on appeal or is anxious to get on with her life (new job, new marriage, etc.) and doesn't want a new trial to hold her back for another year. To avoid the possibility of going back to court, she might give up a few more weekends a year of visitation or may even cut back on some child support money. That does happen on occasion, but the gambit is risky and can cost a lot of time and money.

Although we have examined appeals mostly from the standpoint of a man who has lost his custody trial and is looking for relief, everything here applies to women as well. On those occasions when a man does come out on top and his former spouse files an appeal, he must know that her chances for success are as small as his would be if the roles were reversed.

MODIFICATIONS

Parents will have a much greater chance of success trying to modify a custody, visitation, or child support order. (Technically, alimony can be changed as well, but most agreements do not allow the amount of money and duration of payments to be altered unless the person receiving it gets remarried.) The key is proving to the court that there has been a significant change in circumstances and the modifications are deemed to be in the best interest of the children. If, for example, your income has risen twenty percent or more, your ex-wife could easily argue that she is entitled to a comparable increase in child support. Relocation, remarriage, and the advent of physical or psychological problems may also lead one party to ask for changes in the existing agreement. Like almost all postjudgments, any moves to modify are heard on a short calendar day, which means that very little time is afforded the hearings.

Most attorneys argue that it doesn't make sense to try to

modify an order immediately (within six months) after a trial unless circumstances have suddenly and drastically changed. Otherwise, a judge will likely say that an appeal is the more appropriate action. It is best to wait until changes have occurred that have significant bearing on the existing arrangement. Some people want to modify on an almost annual basis, and technically that is their right; all court orders and settlements are modifiable, and there is no real limit to when a person can ask to have them changed. Once someone has brought a couple of modifications to the court and lost, however, their chances of ever succeeding with that process are remote. Judges simply don't want to see people coming back again and again.

The beauty of modifications is that they are not usually as time consuming or expensive as appeals, they have a greater rate of success, and they can address important issues that arise when the lives of two parents change. But they still mean people have to go back to court, which will certainly cause more anxiety for both children and parents. For that reason they should be initiated with great prudence.

RELOCATION

One of the most common reasons parents try to modify a custody and visitation agreement is relocation. Whether getting remarried, taking on a new job, or looking for a new start in life, the custodial parent may want to move to a different town or state and take the children with him or her. "I have seen a significant increase in the number of custody cases being opened up again because fathers and mothers want to relocate," says Dr.

Stephen Herman, a psychiatrist in New York City who often weighs in as an expert witness on cases such as these . "It is a very complicated issue. The focus must be on the children and what's best for them. But it isn't always so easy to figure out." For example, Herman asks, "Is it in the children's best interest to see their mother fulfill herself with a great new job in Arizona even if it means leaving behind the father in New York, who argues, 'But my children need me, too'?" Even Solomon would have a hard time finding the right answer to that question.

Relocation cases can be as emotionally painful and gut-wrenching as they are complex. Consider the Virginia couple who divorced in 1988 and worked out an amicable custody arrangement in which their two boys stayed with their father from Friday evening through Monday morning three weekends a month. The father also shared alternate holidays with his sons and had them for a block of four weeks in the summer. Three years after the divorce, however, the mother met a man from Oregon on a Club Med vacation and, after dating long-distance for several months, decided to marry him. She told her ex-husband right away, and then announced that she and the boys would be moving to Oregon at the end of the school year, which was only a month away.

The father hired an attorney and immediately tried to get a temporary restraining order preventing her from leaving with their children. The docket was loaded the day they went into court, however, and they could get the judge to devote only ten minutes to the case, after which he ruled that the mother be allowed to move pending a full-fledged hearing on the matter in September.

The hearing took place as scheduled, and after three days of testimony, a different judge said the boys could stay with their mother. The father was devastated that the children, with whom he had contact on a regular basis, would not be able to see him nearly so often. What hurt him most in this case was the initial decision, which had allowed the children to establish roots in Oregon even before the case could be fully heard. It made it that much easier for the mother to argue that the boys should make the move with her, even though they had a solid relationship with their father.

The burden of proof in a relocation case is on the person who wants to move. She has to prove why it is essential that she leave town, even if that means the children's relationship with the other parent will be compromised. As for the individual trying to stop the move, he must demonstrate that it is not necessary and show that the children will suffer without having both parents nearby. "I really need to see that the relocation is in the best interest of the children," says one east coast family court judge. "The overriding consideration is how it will affect the kids." Adds another jurist: "One of the main determinants for me is the history of the parties before the proposed relocation and who has been there for the children. If the person asking you to halt the move is a caring, loving parent who has sacrificed in different ways for his children, then I will view him much differently than one who has always put his job and recreational interests over his kids." But there are other factors, the judge says. "I do not permit relocation when it's the whim of a custodial parent, an attempt for a change of scenery, a change of luck," he explains. "And I don't go for it if it's only to get where there are other members of his or her family. If both parents have been very involved as parents, I am likely to rule against the relocation and maintain the children's access to both."

Figuring out how any judge is going to rule on a relocation case is difficult to do, and although the burden of proof is supposed to be on the person trying to move, some courts are becoming more flexible in their interpretations. As we discussed in chapter 1, twenty-two state supreme courts have handed down rulings since 1985 that were more favorable to the custodial parent who wanted to move far away (200 miles or more), even if it made it harder for the other parent to see the child. In New York, for example, the relocating parent no longer has to prove that the move is necessary because of health reasons, for example, or a job transfer. Although the courts there do insist that any move be "in the best interest of the children," they also add that it is "unrealistic" to try to preserve the noncustodial parent's close involvement in the children's everyday life at the expense of the custodial parent's efforts to start a new life. That is a frightening development for the noncustodial parent who greatly values his time with his kids. His best hope for success is being an integral and irreplaceable part of his children's lives. And if the mother does move, he can always consider relocating himself. That would surely be in the best interests of the kids.

REMARRIAGE AND NEW RELATIONS

A new husband or wife can have a significant impact on a custody arrangement, and so can a postdivorce boyfriend or girlfriend. Say a man's former spouse remarries and her new mate is dealing drugs out of their home, hanging around with unsavory people, or being physically or mentally abusive to the kids; the father has the right to petition the court for modification of custody, and his chances of success in those situations are good as long as he can show the court just how adversely the new relationship could impact the children. You must keep in mind, however, that a woman can raise the same issues about you. Consequently, you should be careful about who you choose to get involved with and what you do together. You should pass on anyone who seems suspect and get to know a new love interest fairly well before introducing her to the children.

What's not so clear is how you should deal with those additions, whether new husbands or boyfriends, who aren't so obviously unfit. Our recommendation is that you keep tabs on the situation by recording things you see and learn about the man in a journal. If a worrisome pattern emerges, you should consult your attorney. Perhaps he'll recommend that you talk to your former spouse about your concerns, or maybe you'll have no choice but to head back to court and secure a modification. Be warned: A judge is not going to alter an agreement simply because a man is not happy with his ex-wife's new mate. The court needs to see and hear substantive evidence that he is truly having an adverse effect on your children's lives before it will make any moves.

VISITATION

Few things are as important to the children of divorce—and their noncustodial parents—as visitation. It gives them both the opportunity to continue their relationship and, as Dr. Stephen Herman points out in his book, *Parent vs. Parent*, is critical to the children's psychological development. It also gives the custodial father or mother a much-needed respite from the rigors of every day single parenting. If that person, however, interferes with visitation in any way, she runs the risk of doing significant emotional damage to the kids. Dr. Herman argues that the removal of one parent from the life of the children because the former couple is unable to set up or adhere to a reasonable visitation schedule is a profound loss that can cause youngsters to feel sad, confused, anxious, and uncertain. It is essential, therefore, that as long as the noncustodial parent does not present any physical or emotional risk to the children, the parent who has custody do whatever he or she can to encourage the participation and presence of the other.

Unfortunately, visitation is perhaps the greatest weapon of the postjudgment battlefield. Custodial parents are forever holding back their children from visitation, or doing whatever they can to make the process extremely difficult for their former spouses. We've heard countless tales from men who have gone to their ex-wives' homes at prescribed times to pick up their children, only to find the house empty and no children in sight. Phone calls are not answered or returned. Schedules are changed at the last minute. Children are dropped off late or picked up early. It is one of the cruelest and most selfish tacks a former spouse can take, especially because it inflicts damage on both the children and the parent. But that doesn't stop people from using it all the time.

So how does a noncustodial parent deal with that issue? Start by making sure visitation is clearly spelled out in the divorce or custody agreement. Some men have accepted "reasonable" visitation, only to learn that their ex-wives' definition of that word is much different from their own. Insist that specific times and dates be put into the document so that everybody is protected. If that, however, doesn't prevent a mother from violating the visitation arrangement, we recommend that you first speak directly to her, without the children being present. You should discuss the harm the behavior is causing your offspring and stress the importance of sticking with a sensible schedule. If that doesn't work, and in many cases it probably won't, court is often the only other option available. The problem with that is twofold. If you bring your ex-wife back before the judge as a result of visitation violations, you will probably have to pick up her legal bills and run the risk of opening yourself up to further claims for alimony and child support. And chances are the courts won't really do much to help remedy the situation. Withhold child support in this day and age, and the legal system snaps to attention. But nothing much happens when visitation is withheld, and judges generally don't put a lot of pressure on parents to conform with the schedule that was laid out. Some even seem to view visitation as some sort of luxury. It's a tragic response to a horrendous problem, and the ones who bear the brunt of such selfish behavior is, of course, the kids.

Some progress is being made in that area, however. The state of Virginia, for example, has started punishing mothers who block children from seeing their dads by stripping them of their custody rights and handing the kids over to their fathers. Illinois, Missouri, and Texas are among those states that have made interference with visitation a low-level criminal offense, and more will likely follow. In the absence of those types of legal reforms, some courts have allowed lawyers to appoint a "monitor" to cases where there are visitation disputes—either a therapist or the attorney for the children involved—who stays in touch with the parents after a divorce or custody case has been resolved and tries to keep them both from using visitation as a way to get back at each other. The advantage of that method is that it puts someone in charge of the problem yet saves everybody the time, money, and risks of having to go back to court. It does not have the legal teeth of, say, a contempt order. Still, employing a monitor, who will charge an hourly rate, is a lot more useful than doing nothing, and you might be wise to anticipate visitation problems by insisting you and your former wife agree to have one on call once your custody agreement takes effect. You should even offer to pay for it if that's what it takes to make it happen; a monitor will be more cost-effective than having to hire a lawyer down the road, and he could become an important independent witness should the violations get so bad that you have to take your ex-wife back to court.

MONEY

Earlier in this chapter we discussed how increases in income can lead to modifications of child support, and the example we used involved a man who ended up paying twenty percent more money to his former wife after his earnings increased by that amount. That seems a fair practice—as long as it is applied equally to women. But the fact is, it's often not. Stories abound of mothers who go to back to work after divorce and custody cases have been settled, and even though their incomes have increased dramatically, they are able to thwart the efforts of their former spouses who want to reduce the child support money they must pay out each month. Your best bet in a situation like that is to work out a reasonable arrangement with your ex-wife that would either lower your monthly bill or give you more time with the kids. If neither of those are possible, the only other recourse is going back to court, which may well be a waste of time and money unless you get a judge who is inclined to treat men and women the same way.

The deck can also be stacked against the man who wants to reduce his child support payments because his income has decreased. We know of a former doctor who was making $200,000 a year when he and his wife divorced. She received primary custody of their two children—daughters, ages eight and ten—and his monthly support payments were based on that rather hefty salary. A couple of years after the divorce was final, however, the forty-two-year-old doctor decided to slow down. He didn't like his job as much anymore, he was tired of all the hours he had to put in, and he wanted to spend more time with his daughters. So he shut down his practice and began teaching at a nearby college. The change suited him well, and his girls relished the extra time they got to share with their father. But when he went to the court and tried to reduce his child support payments–his income had been cut in half–the judge turned him down flat and said he had to continue paying the amount that had been determined by his previous income. Again, the moral here is don't assume the courts will treat you fairly when it comes to money. You shouldn't do anything that will drastically reduce your income–and your ability to meet your obligations–without seeing how your ex-wife will react and getting a sense from your lawyer as to how the local courts will handle the matter.

There are times, of course, when a serious reduction in a man's income is not a matter of choice. Layoffs and firings are a fact of life these days. Problems can also arise as a result of long-term illness, be it physical or psychological in nature. Given the heightened sensitivity to the collection of child support money, you need to act quickly if you find that you cannot make your child support payments. File a motion to modify your obligations downward as soon as possible and don't let the problem go untreated or you could find yourself in trouble with the law. It's not unusual for fathers who fall behind in their payments to lose some, if not all, of their visitation rights.

One more thing about money: We often hear about men who have withheld child support payments as a sort of punishment for ex-wives who have compromised their visitation time. Tempting as that may be, don't do it. We understand a father's anger and frustration in those situations, but holding back money legally due a former spouse will only exacerbate the situation and cause the same sort of legal problems mentioned earlier. Do whatever you can to remedy the situation through negotiations with your former spouse or the court, but keep writing those monthly checks until the courts tell you other-wise.

The idea of going back to court after a long and painful divorce or custody battle is abhorrent to most reasonable people, and well it should be. A legal fight is an emotionally and financially taxing process, and no one in their right mind would want to jump back into that ring again. There are times, however, when the actions of a former spouse leave a person no choice, such as a mother trying to relocate with the children, or an ex-wife denying the basic visitation rights of the noncustodial parent. Then it makes perfect sense to act. Again, you must play to win because there is no other way to fight the battle. But you must always keep in mind the best interests of your children, be aware of what another round of depositions, continuances, and hearings will do to their already fragile psyches, and do what you can to minimize the damage a new legal face-off can bring.

8

WHAT TO DO ONCE YOU GET CUSTODY

EVEN AFTER A CUSTODY CASE HAS ENDED, A PARENT'S overriding consideration must still be what's best for the children. If you have prevailed in your fight, the first thing you have to realize is that taking proper care of the kids on a full-time basis will not be easy. Chances are, however, you already know that. You have likely spent days, weeks, and months on your own with the children and understand the rigors of getting homework done on time, of making sure meals are eaten and baths are taken, of shuttling kids to ballet classes and soccer practices, and of organizing sleepovers, play dates, and birthday parties. A good father also knows that children who have been the object of nasty legal scraps will likely be suffering from the effects of those battles long after they have been fought. And he appreciates that, more than anything else, his kids need to feel truly loved once the conflict is over and deserve to have a strong sense of comfort, stability, and security wherever they may live.

To help ensure that, you must take your children's needs and desires into account each time you make a decision and understand how the things you do will affect them. Turning the kids over to a nanny six days a week won't do them much good, and neither will bringing a different woman over for dinner every Saturday night. To be sure, you need to make some time for yourself, whether it's playing golf with the guys or going to the movies with a steady girlfriend. But you must also make sure that your first priority is taking good care of your kids, for the man who fought for his children has to be there for them after the battle has been won. You argued that you would be the better parent; now you need to show the court–and most importantly the kids–that you were right.

DEALING WITH YOUR FORMER SPOUSE

Perhaps the best thing you can do for your children is put aside your differences with your former spouse and try to deal with her in as civil and constructive a way as possible. No one expects you to suddenly become best friends with your ex-wife. But replacing the rancor of a court fight with a sense of respect and understanding will go a long way toward relieving much of the stress the children have felt throughout the legal process and give them a chance to grow up without some of the emotional problems that often afflict kids who have been the subject of custody disputes. It's essential that although you and your ex-wife may not have be able to live together as husband and wife, you can at least find a way to raise your children with some semblance of cooperation and put the bitterness of the past behind you. Doing so would demonstrate that you love your kids more than you hate each other. That's something the children need to see.

Admittedly, it's not easy to work with a woman you have just battled in court, and vice versa. But the benefits for the kids, and ultimately yourself, can be enormous. Consider the California couple who divorced after four years of marriage and one child. They went through two difficult custody fights before finally settling on an arrangement that had their daughter spending the school year with her father and the summer and most other vacations with the mother, who had moved to the Midwest. The parents both had serious personal issues with each other, but they managed to put them all aside when it came to dealing with their daughter. The two of them communicated well in that regard and looked out for her best interests. When it was time for their daughter to go from one home to the other, the parents always tried to spend a day or two together during the exchange in hopes of making the child's transition easier. "We also thought it would be nice to give her some time with both of us," the mother explains. "To be with us together and to see us getting along." One summer, the parents decided to stretch their layover time to a weekend. "My ex-wife and I got along pretty well," the father says. "We didn't act like lovers, or even ex-lovers, but more like old friends. We could tell that our daughter really enjoyed it. We made it clear to her that we weren't thinking of getting back together, and nothing would come of the visit. But that didn't seem to bother her in the least. As I got ready to fly back to California, she gave me a big hug and said with a bright smile, 'Daddy, I really do have a family.' It seemed to mean so much to her to see us all together, even for a little while. And more important, I think, was my daughter knowing that although her mother and I didn't live together any more, we still had a good relationship that was free for the most part of any real tension. That hadn't been destroyed by the divorce, and that's probably what made our daughter feel that her family hadn't been destroyed either."

Knowing what not to do once a custody battle has ended is just as important as understanding what is right. For example, you should never put down your former spouse in front of the children or make her look bad in any way. Not only does that cause undue stress for the kids, who have already had enough emotional battering to last a lifetime, but it can also give them a terrible image of their mother, which will be even more harmful in the long run. We have a friend who has primary custody of twin nine-year-old girls, and he goes out of his way to praise his ex-wife's part-time career as a dance instructor, even though he wishes she had a better job and contributed more money to their children's upbringing. He realizes that his daughters' primary image of what being a woman is all about, of what they themselves will be all about, comes from the female role model in their lives, their mother. Why, he thinks, would I even consider saying anything derogatory about my former spouse's work situation in front of my daughters when it could only hurt them? Such magnanimous behavior puzzles many of his friends and often drives his family crazy. "They are very critical of my ex-wife and think I should be as well," the father says. "But we're talking about my children's mother, and I can't imagine anything crueler than trying to make her look bad in their eyes. It would only hurt them." But what if the woman had really serious problems? "Then I don't think it's my place to point it out to my children unless things get so bad that it affects their ability to visit and spend time with her," he explains. "Otherwise, they would probably resent me. The children have to make their own decisions about their mother. Obviously, I would be happy to talk with them if they have any questions, but the last thing I want to do is impose my feelings about my former spouse on them."

What should you do if the situation is reversed and your ex-wife is bad-mouthing you in front of the children? Once again, we recommend that you talk to your former spouse first, explaining how harmful it is to the kids and asking her to stop. If that doesn't work, you should go back to the judge and file a motion for contempt of court.

Unfortunately, many fathers who have come out on top in a custody battle have no interest in treating their former spouses with respect or understanding. Instead, they seem intent on making their ex-wives suffer further by taking every opportunity they get to hurt them more. It may be holding the kids back from visitation. It could be flaunting a new relationship. It might even come in the form of verbal jabs constantly reminding the mother that she lost the custody case. It's understandable how people can think of acting that way. Few things are as emotionally charged as a divorce or custody battle, and the residual pain and anger can fuel the desire for revenge. But nothing really excuses that kind of conduct. First of all, there's no point in destroying another person emotionally, especially when it's the mother of your children, someone your kids are going to be spending a lot of time with. It's better to have a strong, confident, and capable former spouse who can be a good role model for your children and coparent effectively. A woman whose sense of self has been thoroughly destroyed by a custody battle may hardly be able to take care of herself, much less the kids on the occasions she has them.

You will also find that the sooner you get over the battle you fought with your ex-wife, the quicker you can get on with your life. Nothing can be more destructive to your psyche than lugging around a ton of anger and resentment and expending most of your energy trying to get back at someone you feel has done you wrong. The fight is over, and the marriage is done. You must act that way.

Some men argue that there's nothing to be gained by taking the high road in dealing with a former spouse, but we disagree. In addition to being the best thing for the children in the vast majority of the cases, it also gives the man reason to feel good about himself and know that he is doing the right thing. Trite as it may seem, that's important for a father who has been through a messy divorce and custody dispute. The emotional toll of such a battle is enormous, and it often takes months to recover. One way to speed up that process is to start feeling good about yourself again. Another is to give up the fight once the fight has ended and move on to the next stage of your relationship with your former wife and the children who are now in your custody.

Learning how to deal with an ex-wife is of paramount importance to a man who has just weathered a divorce or custody dispute, but there are several other issues you must also contend with as you try to figure out life after court. What about moving?

Or remarrying? How do you deal with visitation and the problems that often arise from it? And how do you keep up relations with your wife's family, who will likely want to see the kids as well?

MOVING

The temptation is often there when the fighting has stopped to pull up stakes and leave town. Sometimes, you simply want a change of scenery for yourself and your family, and that is understandable. There is something about a terrible divorce or custody battle that makes people want to find a place where no sour memories linger and where the anguish of a horrendous court fight is not so easily felt. Or perhaps it's a new job or the opportunity to move where the roads are less crowded, the prices a bit lower, and the pace of life a little more relaxed. Those are perfectly natural reactions, but the man who has won custody must be very careful about acting on any of them.

First of all, changing locations rarely changes anything about a person's plight. The man who is troubled in Texas will likely feel that same way should he move to New Hampshire. So that's not the right reason to go, especially if it means uprooting the children from a community in which they have important relationships with friends and family. You would be much wiser to stay in town and give your kids some much-deserved continuity. And you might find things getting better for yourself if you take time to decompress after the court case and adjust to life as a single dad.

But what if there's an offer of an exciting new job? Or if you have the chance to take your family to a place where the quality of life is better? Those, too, must be examined closely, for as the primary parent you should always try and do what you can to improve your children's lives. But at the same time, you should avoid making any moves or decisions that would compromise the kids' relationship with a loving and nurturing mother. Few things are as painful as the relocation of a family at the expense of a noncustodial parent who suddenly finds herself cut off from regular contact with the children. The hurt is probably even worse for the kids. So although the desires of those who want to move are understandable, we believe that mothers or fathers who do move far away from perfectly good parents are probably doing their children a grave disservice. Generally speaking, young boys and girls do much better emotionally when they have regular contact with both their parents, and it simply isn't fair to upset their relationship with the noncustodial parent. In fact, we view most such moves as extremely selfish and would encourage parents who have primary custody to think long and hard before trying to take children away from a loving ex-spouse. To be sure, relocation to a neighboring county or town may have minimal impact, but anything more than that is hard to countenance.

If you must move with your kids, it's important to handle that decision in the proper way. First of all, you shouldn't leave in the middle of the night without telling anybody else. Not only could that cause significant psychological damage to the children, but it would also put you in serious trouble with the law and would almost certainly result in losing custody once you are found out. The best thing to do is talk with your former spouse about your desire to move and see if she would agree to it. Perhaps the mother will see the benefit in the relocation and will consent to it if some provisions are made to allow plenty of visitation time (and maybe even some help with transportation costs, etc.). Who knows, she might even consider moving herself in an effort to maintain close relations. If she doesn't want you to move on any circumstances, however, your only option is going back to court and seeking its permission.

NEW RELATIONSHIPS, NEW MARRIAGES

These are facts of life for most men and women after divorce, and they can have a profound effect on the children involved. The best advice we can offer is, take it slow. The impulse to hook up with someone else right away is strong, as people who suddenly find themselves on their own look to put a family back together and rebuild the home they lost when their marriage fell apart. But don't try to fix it all at once. You should get used to being back on your own and give yourself some time to heal after your divorce and custody battle. The kids need this, too. Dating is fine so long as you aren't bringing different women home each weekend and employing an army of baby sitters to take care of your children while you're out on the town. You need to remember that, as the primary custodial parent, you have different responsibilities, and those can certainly put a damper on your social life. For one thing, there should be no sleepovers with the children present unless there is reason to believe that the woman spending the night might one day be their stepmother. As for introducing the kids to a new love inter-

est and involving her in family outings and activities, we recommend that you first make sure the relationship is solid and
has some staying power. You don't want to introduce them to
someone who might well be out of the picture in another
month. Parading a slew of strangers in and out of the children's
lives can only prove harmful, especially as they try to recover
from their parents' divorce and get used to living mostly without one parent.

Next, you should talk with your kids about meeting your new
girlfriend well before they actually get together for the first
time; springing her on the children one Saturday afternoon will
only invite disaster. Once they have met, you should not be surprised if it takes the kids a while to warm up to the woman.
Dating is as new to them as it is to you, and they are going to be
confused by everything surrounding the process. Who knows,
the kids may even be harboring hopes of their parents reunit-
ing, which can cause further resentment. The important thing is
to handle the situation with great sensitivity and give the children time to accept and to adjust.

Look closely at the long-term effects of a new relationship
and whether it really has all the right components for a good
marriage before getting too deeply involved. Face it, people who
have been divorced before have proven that their judgment of
the opposite sex is not always sound, and they need to be extra
cautious the second time around, both for their sake and for
their kids'. Keep an eye out for signs of trouble. Does she drink
too much? Is she good with the children? Is she too possessive?
Does she have her own friends and interests? Does she want a
serious relationship, or would she prefer just to date casually? It

is essential to take the time to really get to know a serious love interest; anyone can put up a front for a while, but a person's true colors—as well as their fears and insecurities—will eventually show over a period of months or even years.

A single father will find the going rough on occasion because some women regard the presence of kids as threatening. They will often force a man who has children to make some choices in that regard. We know of several people who have gotten involved with women who initially said they didn't mind sharing time and affections with children but suddenly announced later on that they didn't like the arrangement at all. You should always be up front about your relationship with your kids and how important they are to you. If the woman you are dating has a problem with that, then you should consider finding someone else. That can be a difficult decision to make, but the man who understands his role as a father will work it out.

One final note on this subject: We have talked to a lot of divorced men and women who are enormously cynical about new relationships. In fact, they've become so dismayed about the possibility of finding someone special that they have written off all potential suitors as bums and locked their emotions so deeply away that they have almost lost all capacity to love. That sort of behavior is understandable, to a degree. But the person who refuses to open up again is the person who is going to spend the rest of his life alone. Don't do it. A healthy new relationship can be good for all involved.

THE FORMER SPOUSE'S FAMILY

The in-laws were bad enough during the marriage, but what to do with them after the divorce? The answer is to: make it easy for them to spend time with the children. There is no reason to do anything but encourage those relationships with the mother's family, unless, of course, they are causing serious problems. It's the best thing for all involved, not only for the time it gives them together but also for the nonconfrontational tone it can set for the postdivorce relationship. And it certainly wouldn't hurt you to have some extra free time on those occasions when your former mother-in-law takes the children to the library. Any sane single parent would appreciate the break.

VISITATION

One of the most important parts about being a good custodial father is adhering to both the letter and spirit of the visitation agreement so that the children have unfettered access to their mother. As Dr. Stephen Herman explains in his book, *Parent* vs. *Parent*, a child's ability to heal and rebound after a divorce and custody dispute is directly related to frequent and unimpeded access to both parents. There are few things more scurrilous than a father who holds children back from seeing his former spouse for no good reason. It is damaging to both emotionally and can quickly turn an amicable postdivorce relationship into a full-fledged war. You should never stoop to that level. If you have a problem with your ex-wife and the visitation arrangement or the way the exchanges are being handled, then you should speak with her when the children are not around and attempt to work something out. If the trouble persists, or you feel that visitation should be curtailed or modified in some way, take care of it through the proper legal channels.

Most parents have a hard time with visitation and complain about how awkward it feels to be passing their children back and forth with their former spouses. Imagine, then, how the kids feel. It wasn't too long ago that their seemingly happy home included both their mother and father, and now all of a sudden they are commuting between parents who are not only incapable of living together but also have a hard time just getting along. According to Dr. Herman, there are several things a custodial parent can do to make things easier for the children. Prepare them for the visit, he explains. Talk about it in advance, and do so in a natural and relaxed way. You should let the kids know that you appreciate how important this time with their mother is, and although you are going to miss them, you hope they have a good time. Do not, Herman emphasizes, speak disparagingly of the parent, and don't pass messages through the child or try to sabotage the visit by making comments such as "Don't worry, you can come home as early as you like." In fact, he recommends that parents not make any telephone calls to their former spouse's house during visitation, unless, of course, there is an emergency.

The University of Connecticut Cooperative Extension System and School of Family Studies has published a teaching guide for a course entitled "Parenting Apart: Strategies for Effective Co-parenting," and it outlines a series of dos and don'ts for visitation. Be flexible about schedules, it urges. Give the other parent as much advance notice of changes in visitation as possible and provide vacation schedules in advance. Show up on time. And let the other parent know if a new romantic partner or friend will be part of the pick-up. As for the don'ts, the guide recommends that parents not communicate with each other in an uncivil way. It says that children must not be asked to spy on the former spouse, and suggests that parents not use pick-up and drop-off times to try and settle sensitive matters that may lead to fights. Deal with those matters in separate meetings or phone calls without the children being present. And finally, a man should never make his kids feel guilty about spending time with their mother; in fact, he should do everything in his power to make the children feel that it's okay to love Mommy and have a good time with her.

Once the visit is over, most therapists agree that it's best to give the children a chance to make the transition between homes without undue stress and give them an opportunity to readjust. It's fine to ask the kids about their visit in a caring and constructive way, but any sort of interrogation is completely out of line. If you have problems with what went on between your children and their mother, you should take it up with your former spouse and not with the kids.

That's really the main point of this chapter: You need to respect your children's feelings at all times and make sure your actions don't upset them unnecessarily. It's not always the easiest approach for a father, but it is certainly the one that will help your kids weather the divorce and custody battle in the best possible shape.

9

HOW WE CAN FIX THE SYSTEM

LISTEN TO THE MEN WHO HAVE FOUGHT FOR THEIR children, and win or lose, their comments sound the same. "I can't believe how long that trial took," one remarks. "Didn't the judge hear anything I had to say?" another asks. Why were there so many delays? Why was there so much animosity? Why did it cost so much money? Fathers frequently complain about how unfairly the legal system treats them and their children, and in most cases they have every right to. The process is fraught with deficiencies and generally slanted in favor of women. And many times it seems to ignore what is truly in the best interests of the kids.

So how can all that be changed? Thankfully, a transformation of sorts has already begun. For one thing, more and more older judges are retiring. Many judges of that generation left the child rearing up to their wives and simply can't imagine another male in a primary parenting role. Thankfully they are being replaced by younger men and women who are more used to seeing fathers parent and who accept the fathers' roles in the household far more readily. That means there should be less prejudice against men in the courtroom. Secondly, a number of new laws protecting the rights of fathers are being enacted throughout the country. Judges are now forbidding mothers in some venues from relocating out of state with their children if those moves would make it harder for the kids to see their fathers. In addition, courts in several states have been filing criminal charges against mothers who keep children from scheduled visitations with their dads. Some have even gone so far as to take custody away from women if that sort of behavior persists. More than thirty-five states have also ruled that fathers who have their children a significant amount of time, say, more than one hundred nights a year, can reduce their child support payments because they are taking care of their kids so often. Laws in Texas now lower a father's child support payments by basing them on income after taxes and give further discounts to men who have started second families. And the state of New Jersey created a commission to study divorce laws that has recommended, among other things, that a parent who prevents the other from seeing the children be fined and then forced to offer make-up time. Thirdly, there has been a dramatic increase in the number of men filing for custody of their children, whether it is for sole or joint. At the same time, growing public awareness that fathers can parent as well as mothers has led to acceptance of the notion that men deserve equal treatment under the law.

Those are all significant developments, and it's heartening to see them come about. But the fact is, much remains to be done before the legal playing field is leveled. The court system is still rife with problems when it comes to resolving the horrific conflicts that arise during custody battles. Strategies must be found for making sure not only that the children's needs are taken care of but also that the parents who have squared off in court can learn to deal with each other cooperatively in a postdivorce relationship.

Fixing that system is no easy task, but would-be reformers might look to the example set by the statewide custody court in Middletown, Connecticut, where the recently retired Judge Joseph L. Steinberg developed a unique program that takes a lot of the venom out of custody fights. Known as Special Masters, it has been in use since September 1994. Initially, it employed teams of two lawyers (called the Special Masters), a man and a woman each working pro bono, who met with the parents and attorneys involved in a custody case and spent a day trying to get them to settle their dispute. But Steinberg modified the team make-up after only one year, replacing one of the lawyers with a therapist. As far as we know, it's the only program in the country that puts lawyers and therapists together on a pro bono basis to mediate custody disputes. The idea is to prod parents into reaching a workable custody agreement in order to avoid a trial that will almost certainly damage the children further, allow a stranger (the judge) to set up visitation schedules, and make it almost impossible for embittered parents to cooperate in the future.

By all accounts the Special Masters program has worked well. As we pointed out in chapter 4, Steinberg heard 215 cases during the program's first two years, and a remarkable eighty-four percent of them settled before going to trial. Much of that success is a result of the judge's keen understanding and thoughtfulness; a one-time divorce lawyer who spent twenty-five years practicing in the state, he also trained for a time as a family therapist and greatly values the skill and insight a mental health professional brings into a courtroom. But those settlements were also secured because of the Special Masters' ability to peel away the layers of animosity and misconception inherent in custody battles and to get people to focus on what's best for their kids. "It's as innovative a procedure as I've ever seen," says Lisa Faccadio, who has been practicing family law in Connecticut for the past twenty years. Adds Scott Torquato, a clinical social worker and psychotherapist: "I think it's a tremendous program. I've been a firm believer that the law alone is not set up to handle divorce and custody cases and that the behavioral science component was always missing. But Special Masters pairs them beautifully."

The court in Middletown receives only the state's most difficult and seemingly hopeless custody and visitation disputes. Typically, the program begins with a meeting between the judge, the parents, the attorneys, and the lawyer-therapist team (the Special Masters). Steinberg opened with a speech describing how important the issue of custody was and urged the parents to work something out themselves. Then he would leave the rest of the group to watch a seventeen-minute film on the effects of divorce and custody battles on young children. Once that was over, the Special Masters began meeting with the different parties in an attempt to forge an agreement by the close of business that day. If they weren't able to work something out in that time, the Masters were dismissed and a trial date set. But if a settlement appeared imminent, and the Masters agreed, Steinberg extended the process to the following morning.

Opinions vary as to why Steinberg's program works so well. Some attorneys think part of it is the setting; the courthouse is an attractive, modern building that sits right on the banks of the Connecticut River. The conference rooms are comfortable and the atmosphere almost serene, which is a far cry from the crowded chaos of most urban courthouses. "The quality of the venue helps," says attorney Faccadio, "and so does the fact that you have just one day to settle. Everyone is that much more focused because there are no other cases to worry about and no outside delays. We all have time to deal with our clients, with the other litigants, with the children's attorneys, and with the Special Masters. It brings a lot of thoughtfulness, civility, and dignity to a very difficult process." Adds therapist Torquato: "Attorneys know the law, and they have experience in dealing with people at their worst. But they just aren't as good at flushing out the key issues in an interpersonal relationship," which, of course, is the strength of the mental health professional. "The therapist can identify a certain issue and then focus on it so that a whole range of potential problems can emerge," Torquato concludes. "He or she can unstick personal issues so that legal issues can be resolved."

We have observed Judge Steinberg's program in action on many occasions and think it is the most innovative and productive way of dealing with custody cases that we have ever seen. In fact, we would like to see it expanded to include more than just the most troublesome custody cases, and we hope that other states will adopt similar procedures.

Another idea for improving the current system would be to create a panel made up of a judge, a psychologist or psychiatrist, and a layperson that would be charged with making custody decisions. As with the Special Masters, it would be a great benefit to have a person with a strong psychology or social science background helping out. We also like the fact that the ruling wouldn't be left up to just one individual. One Superior Court judge thought the notion made good sense. "We already rely on the input of professionals such as social workers and psychologists in our profession," she says. "It would be a small yet sensible jump having them sit next to us." A worker with Connecticut's Family Services Department adds, "An arrangement like that would present a richer kind of consideration for the situation at hand and lessen the possibility of an inappropriate decision being made."

Another alternative for parents struggling through a custody battle is mediation. Generally, that process centers around the work of an impartial lawyer-therapist team, not unlike the one used in the Special Masters program. In theory, the lawyer is supposed to handle all legal issues, while the therapist takes care of the emotional problems in a cooperative and nonconfrontational way. The goal is to avoid the lengthy and expensive pitfalls of a full-blown legal battle and to reach instead a fair and lasting settlement. In many cases they are able to do just that. In his book, *Parent vs. Parent,* Dr. Stephen Herman cites several studies that speak to the effectiveness of mediation. One conducted in Toronto in the early 1980s shows that only ten percent of mediated couples returned to the courtroom after two years with problems related to custody or visitation, as compared to twenty-six percent of the nonmediated couples. Another from the University of Virginia some years later compared two groups of twenty families each, one of which had chosen mediation and the other litigation. The results showed that mediation had reduced by sixty-seven percent the number of custody disputes that ended up in court; fifteen of the twenty mediating families were able to reach some sort of an agreement while only five of the twenty litigating families reached an out-of-court settlement. Then there is Maine, which is one of only a few states that has established one-time, court-mandated mediation for divorce and custody battles. Only one-quarter of those cases actually goes to litigation, though it is important to point out that the other seventy-five percent are not necessarily resolved; some may go on to further mediation while others may simply put the process on hold for a while.

Anything that reduces the conflict surrounding custody cases and makes it easier for mothers and fathers, and not the courts, to decide where the kids will live and how much time they will spend with each parent seems like a good idea. We think that lawyer-therapist teams have enormous value when it comes to resolving conflicts of this nature, but we still are not completely sold on mediation. First of all, only those couples who can truly cooperate with each other have a prayer of making the process work. Otherwise, it is probably just a waste of time. Secondly, mediation lacks the urgency of the Special Masters program, and there isn't the ominous hammer of a full-blown trial hanging over the parents' heads. One of the things that has made

Steinberg's method so effective is his impressing upon the mothers and fathers before him that he, not they, will be the one deciding the fate of their children if they cannot reach a decision that day. And he lets them both know how troubling he finds it that any parent would let a complete stranger have that sort of control over their kids.

Another problem with mediation is the perceived impartiality of the lawyers and therapists involved. We know of one man who had a respected female lawyer successfully mediate his divorce and then asked her to help resolve a custody dispute several years later. She agreed to take on the case and met with the couple on several occasions. Talks broke down when it became clear that neither side was going to budge, and the man decided to drop the mediator and hire his own attorney. He didn't want a protracted legal battle any more than his former spouse did, but he felt that that was the only way to serve his best interests and those of his children. The mediator was incensed at his actions and accused him of scuttling the talks on purpose. She later helped his ex-wife find a lawyer of her own and then assisted in her case. Ultimately, the man prevailed in his battle, but the mediator's actions prolonged the custody dispute and created an extraordinary amount of stress for all involved. The moral here is, be extremely careful. Mediators work for both parents, not one. And their goal is to come up with a settlement, not to represent the best interests of any one party. Some people are understandably uncomfortable putting their faith and trust in that sort of arrangement, and if that's the case for you, we recommend that you forget about it. But we also suggest that you never forget about the virtues of settling, which can be done just as easily with individual lawyers.

In researching this volume, we spoke with more than fifty sources, and many of them offered their own ideas on how to fix the legal system as it relates to custody and divorce. Following are several of their suggestions, as well as a few more of our own:

1. In 1997, Judge Joseph L. Steinberg organized a five-part lecture series for therapists and lawyers in the state of Connecticut that discussed issues involving families and divorce. It was used primarily as a training exercise for men and women serving as Special Masters but was also opened up to Family Court judges. Using a wide-ranging curriculum, including material from the University of Connecticut's School of Family Studies, it touched on a number of pertinent subjects, such as the effects of divorce and custody disputes on children. The series went a long way toward broadening the participants' views on those subjects, increasing their effectiveness in dealing with the emotional issues that arise as a result of a divorce or custody battle, and giving lawyers and therapists some important common ground that may help them collaborate in the future. Not surprisingly, the course was well attended, and so was one Steinberg put together the year before, a seven-part seminar on child development. The judge believes that courses such as these can go a long way toward improving the nature of the divorce and custody experience for fathers, mothers and their children. We agree, and we would like to see these sorts of annual lecture series mandated through-

out the country. The more people understand the ways that divorce and custody disputes affect children, the better it will be for the children who find their lives turned upside down by them.

2. Divorcing parents in the state of Connecticut may be required by the Judicial Department to attend a three-session course taught by mental health professionals on reorganizing the family once a split has occurred and improving communications between former spouses. The idea is to teach parents who are divorcing or separating new skills to handle not only the stresses and upsets connected with those changes but also to find a way to take good care of their children after the split. It's a terrific program that provides valuable information on how children of different ages react to divorce, for example, and what parents can do to ease their pain. We'd like to see a course like this made mandatory for all parents who are filing for separation or divorce, because it can help them—and their kids—get through those trying times and build strong relationships for the future. It's possible, too, that such a course could even help save some marriages by making people realize the impact their actions will have on the children.

3. We have talked to a number of sources who believe that divorce has become too easy, thanks in large part to no-fault laws. They argue that if it was made more difficult, especially in circumstances in which there are children, then people would work harder on their marriages. One

idea, for example, is to double the mandatory waiting period for a divorce, which is ninety days in many states, and force disgruntled couples to spend more time contemplating their intentions to split and the effects they could have on their children. It's something worth considering.

4.   Several lawyers we spoke to think that mandatory temporary injunctions should be entered in all divorce or custody cases as soon as the initial filing takes place. These injunctions would prevent, for example, either parent from leaving the state with the children for more than a weekend without permission from the other. The goal here is to halt the legal ambush that so often occurs in the beginning stages of a divorce or custody proceeding, before the case has received a full hearing before a judge.

5.   There has been a lot of discussion over the years of child support and its relation to visitation. Many men feel they get the short end of both sticks—minimal visitation and maximum child support—and we appreciate their concerns. It is categorically unfair to expect a man to bear all the financial burdens of his children's upbringing and yet not be allowed to spend appropriate amounts of time with them. Fathers in this position are made to feel more like paychecks than parents, and they are not going to be as involved with their kids or their former spouses as they might be otherwise. To help remedy that situation, courts need to be fairer as they set up support amounts

and visitation schedules and make sure men are given the opportunity to truly participate in their children's lives and not just finance them. If a man begins spending substantially more time with his kids, the amount of money he pays out to his ex-wife each month should be reduced. It seems only fair that if the mother has the children less, the father should not have to pay out as much.

6. "Deadbeat Dads" have been a hot issue in recent years, and few members of society are more reviled than those men who shirk their financial responsibilities to their children. And rightly so if they have the money and it is being withheld out of greed, disdain, or malice. But people need to have a much deeper understanding of why some men stop paying child support. It may be the result of financial problems associated with a job loss or the heavy burden of trying to keep up with substantial alimony and support payments, and there's not much they can do about it. At least not right away. We have heard countless stories of judges who have jailed fathers for falling behind on their commitments, even if it was because of a sudden layoff or some similar problem. We also know of men who have switched to jobs with lower salaries and then had the courts refuse to adjust their support payments accordingly. It would be better if the legal system treated men in those situations with a modicum of understanding and not rush to judgment so quickly. Give them a chance to find new work. Understand why they opted for a lower-paying job. Let

them pay what they can afford. But throwing them behind bars serves only to make the men feel lousier about themselves, push them further away from their children, and inflame an already volatile relationship with their former spouses.

In fact, we would like to see a societal change in attitude regarding so-called "Deadbeat Dads," because the perception of fathers who fall behind in their support payments or who stop altogether is neither accurate nor fair. Consider that a recent Health and Human Services report to Congress revealed that sixty-six percent of those fathers who cannot comply with support orders are in that position because of unemployment or underemployment. Nearly eight percent can't pay because they are locked up in jail, and another six percent are unable to fork over their share because they are deceased. That's right, some 600,000 dead men are included in the government's numbers on dads who aren't paying their child support. Take out the men in prison and the ones who are no longer with us, and the total number of fathers who have defaulted on their support payments falls from 3 million to 1.7 million. And that total is only a little bit higher than the 1.3 million women who have defaulted on their support commitments.

In addition, it would be good to see the courts enforce violations of visitation agreements as vigorously as non-payments of support. Infringing on the ability of a parent to spend time with his children is just as egregious, but it is rarely treated that way by judges. It certainly doesn't stir the ire of society in the same way. But what can possibly be worse than a parent using a child to get back at a former spouse or than keeping a child from his father? We applaud those states that mete out punishment to parents who prevent their former spouses from seeing their children. We do not advocate the withholding of child support–that only serves to hurt the child; but we are not opposed to the filing of criminal charges against a mother who interferes with a father's right to spend time with his children, and we like the idea of taking custody away from a woman who persists in the practice.

7. One therapist we spoke with believes the legal system needs better-educated judges. "I have been surprised and appalled by the level of competence I have seen over the years," he says. "Many of the judges I have dealt with don't know a thing about children or the dynamics of a family, yet they're the ones making these enormously important decisions. I would like to mandate a sort of continuing education for judges that teaches them about family violence, child psychology, things of that sort. Such classes would better equip them to handle divorce and custody cases and to be more sensitive to the needs and emotional impact of the children involved."

8. With regard to judges and other members of the court and to the state judicial system involved in the custody process, a social worker we know says: "I don't think anyone who doesn't have children should be making

decisions in a custody case. If you don't have kids, you aren't going to understand the situation nearly as well, and I think you would be handicapped as a result."

There are many ways to fix the system that is in place today, and all of the changes suggested above have merit. There are likely many others that could be made as well. Whatever the specifics, the important thing is that we take as much of the confrontation as possible out of the system and make sure the system truly serves the best interests of the children. They didn't ask to be brought into this world, and they certainly didn't ask to have their quiet and comfortable routines torn apart by a divorce or custody battle. Anything we can do to help them get through those tough times and go on to lead happy and secure lives would be worth it.

INDEX

A

Aggressiveness of lawyer, 32
Alimony, modification of, 119–20
American Academy of Matrimonial
    Lawyers as source of lawyer, 28
American Association for Mediated
    Divorce, 36–37
American Divorce Association for
    Men, 164
American Divorce Association of
    Men (ADAM), 164
American Fathers Coalition, 5–6
American Society of Separated and
    Divorced Men, 164
Appeals, 116–19
Arizona Fathers' Rights, 164
Attorney. See Lawyer

B

Babysitter, avoiding use of, 39
Barnes, Scott and Missy, case study
    of, 108–13
Best interests doctrine, xx, 67–68, 69
Birdnesting, 71
Bryan, Eric and Martha, case study
    of, 102–8
Bryant, Jim, 13
Burden of proof in relocation case,
    122–23

C

California, relocation rulings in, 16
California United Fathers, 164
Career as problem in custody fight,
    13–15
Case studies, 93–94
    Barnes case, 108–13
    Bryan case, 102–8
    Johnson case, 94–97
    Paine case, 97–102
Character witnesses in custody trial,
    61, 90
Children
    age-appropriate treatment of,
        52–53
    bracing, for custody fight, 37–38,
        52–54
    communication with lawyer, 33
    fighting for rights to parent,
        21–23
    impact of custody fight on, 22–23,
        38, 131–32
    impact of joint custody on, 69–71
    impact of parent relationships on,
        132–37
    importance of, in initiation of legal
        action, 46–48
    legal representation for, 33, 51,
        54–55

Helpful Organizations

American Divorce Association
of Men (ADAM)
1519 S. Arlington Heights Rd.
Arlington Heights, IL 60005
847-364-1555

American Divorce
Association for Men
1008 White Oak St.
Arlington Heights, IL 60005
312-870-1040

American Society of
Separated and Divorced Men
575 Keep St.
Elgin, IL 60120
847-695-2200

Arizona Fathers' Rights
P.O. Box 30894
Mesa, AZ 85275
602-830-0744

California United Fathers
6360 Van Nuys Blvd., No. 8
Van Nuys, CA 91401
818-785-1440

Concerned Fathers
P.O. Box 2768
Springfield, MA 01564
413-736-7432

Dads Against Discrimination
P.O. Box 8525
Portland, OR 97207
503-222-1111

Divorced Men's Association
P.O. Box 380576
East Hartford, CT 06138
860-568-7742

Domestic Rights Coalition
1849 E. Iowa St.
St. Paul, MN 55119
612-774-7010

Equal Rights for Divorced
    Fathers
Urga Building
302 E. Charleston, No. 204
Reno, NV 89509
702-387-6266.

Family Re-entry
520 West Ave
Norwalk, CT 06851
203-838-0496

Fathers Are Forever
P.O. Box 4804
Panorama City, CA 91412
818-846-2219

Fathers for Equal Rights, Inc.
3623 Douglas Ave.

Des Moines, IA 50310
515-277-8789

Fathers for Equal Rights
P.O. Box 010847
Flagler Station
Miami, FL 33101
305-895-6351.

Fathers for Equal Rights
1210 E. Colfax, No. 306
Denver, CO 80218
303-831-7853

Fathers Helping Fathers
170-B Pleasant Street
South Yarmouth, MA 02665
508-760-2045

Fathers Helping Fathers
46 Old Ashby Rd.
Greenville, NH 03048
603-878-3279

Fathers Rights and Equality
    Exchange
3140 De La Cruz Blvd.,
Suite 200

Santa Clara, CA 95054
415-853-6877

Fathers United for Equal
   Rights, Ltd.
P.O. Box 511
Randallstown, MD 21133
410-764-9340

Joint Custody Association
10606 Wilkins Ave.
Los Angeles, CA 90024
213-475-5352

National Organization for
   Men
381 Park Avenue South
New York, NY 10016
212-766-4030

Male Parents for Equal Rights
600 Wildel Ave., No. 67
New Castle, DE 19720-6136
302-571-8383

Men's Rights Association
17854 Lyons
Forest Lake, MN 55025
612-464-7887

Parents Sharing Custody
420 S. Beverly Dr., Suite 1000
Beverly Hills, CA 90212
310-286-9171

Parents Without Partners
401 N. Michigan Ave.
Chicago, IL 60611
312-644-6610

Texas Fathers' Alliance
P.O. Box 12393
Austin, TX 78711
512-472-3237

United Fathers
12304 Santa Monica Blvd.
Santa Monica, CA 90025
310-442-8575

United Fathers of America
595 The City Dr., Suite 202
Orange, CA 92668
714-385-1002.

Wisconsin Fathers for Equal
   Justice
2116 Monroe St.
Madison, WI 53711
608-255-1100